# THE
# HBCU
# EXPERIENCE

## THE HBCU BAND ALUMNI 3rd EDITION

Visionary Author: Dr. Ashley Little
Lead Author: Dr. Christy A. Walker
Foreword Author: Dr. Roderick Little
Foreword Author: Shonnie Murrell

Published By: The HBCU Experience Movement, LLC

The HBCU Experience Movement, LLC

thehbcuexperiencemovement@gmail.com

Ordering Information:
Quantity Sales: Special discounts are available on quantity purchases by corporations, associations, and nonprofits. For details, contact the publisher at the address above.

ISBN: 979-8-218-27440-5

# DR. ASHLEY LITTLE

# A Message from the Founder
## Dr. Ashley Little

Historically Black Colleges & Universities (HBCUs) were established to serve the educational needs of black Americans. During the time of their establishment, and many years afterward, blacks were generally denied admission to traditionally white institutions. Prior to The Civil War, there was no structured higher education system for black students. Public policy, and certain statutory provisions, prohibited the education of blacks in various parts of the nation. Today, HBCUs represent a vital component of American higher education.

*The HBCU Experience Movement, LLC* is a collection of stories from prominent alumni throughout the world, who share how their HBCU experience molded them into the people they are today. We are also investing financially into HBCUs throughout the country. Our goal is to create a global movement of prominent HBCU alumni throughout the nation to continue to share their stories each year, allowing us to give back to prestigious HBCUs annually.

We are proud to present to you *The HBCU Experience: The HBCU Band Alumni 3rd Edition*. We would like to acknowledge and give special thanks to our amazing lead author/partner, Dr. Christy A.Walker, for your dedication and commitment. We appreciate you and thank you for your hard work and dedication on behalf of this project. We would also like to give a special thanks to our foreword authors, expert authors, contributing authors and partners for believing in this movement and investing your time, and monetary donations, to give back to your school. We appreciate all of the The HBCU Band Alumni who shared your HBCU experience in the HBCU Band Alumni 3rd Edition publication.

## About Dr. Ashley Little

Dr. Ashley Little is Ms. Global Continental 2023 and the CEO/Founder of Ashley Little Enterprises, LLC, which encompasses her media, consulting work, writing, ghost writing, book publishing, book coaching, project management, magazine, public relations & marketing, and empowerment speaking. In addition, she is an award-winning serial entrepreneur, TV/radio host, TEDx speaker, international speaker, keynote speaker, media maven, journalist, writer, host, philanthropist, business coach, investor, advisor for She Wins Society, and 21-times award-winning bestselling author. As seen on Black Enterprise (2X), *Forbes* (2X), *Sheen* Magazine (Print and Online), Sheen Talk, Voyage ATL, Fox Soul TV, NBC, Fox, CBS, BlackNews.Com, Shoutout Miami, Shoutout Atlanta, Morning Star, Yahoo Finance, Heart and Soul, The Book of Sean, *HBCU Times*, *VIP Global Magazine*, The Black Report, Vocal, Ted.com, Medium, Soul Wealth, Hustle and Soul, BlackBusiness.com, Glambitious Top 21 Women Of 2021, New York Weekly's Top 10 Hardest Working CEOs alongside billionaire Mark Cuban, *US Insider's* Top 10 Women Entrepreneurs alongside billionaire and media mogul, Oprah Winfrey, *London Daily Post*, *Sheen* Magazine 5 Pioneers Making a Difference in Their Communities, NCA&T *Alumni Times*, CEO Weekly Top 10 Influential People in 2021 alongside billionaires Jeff Bezos and Beyonce' and many more. Through the Biden & Harris Administration, and Leaders Esteem Christian Bible University, she was also awarded with the Presidential Lifetime Achievement Award. She is a board member for Leaders Esteem Christian Bible University, as well.

As a recipient of the "Author of The Year" award by Glambitious, she is also a part of The Forbes Next 1000 Class of 2021 in partnership with Square. This first-of-its-kind initiative celebrates bold and inspiring entrepreneurs who are redefining what it means to run a business. Furthermore, she was a recipient of Nashville's Black 40 Under 40 Awards in December 2021. It is an annual event honoring the best and the brightest for their accomplishments in their chosen field and for their contributions and commitment to the African American community. Dr. Little is also an official member of For(bes) The Culture. For(bes) The Culture was formed in Boston at the Forbes Under 30 Summit in October of 2017. They pride themselves on convening current and future black and brown leaders worldwide to network, collaborate, share opportunities, and discuss issues related to their communities and the planet at-large. She was recognized along with other influential leaders and distinguished entrepreneurs, including Oprah Winfrey, Mel Robbins, Gary V and many more for the annual Brainz 500 Global Awards List awarded by *Brainz* Magazine. Lastly, she is a proud member of The Chancellor's Round Table at North Carolina A&T State University.

She is a proud member of Delta Sigma Theta Sorority, Incorporated, and a member of Alpha Phi Omega. She is very involved in her community, organizations and non-profits. Currently, she is the co-founder of Sweetheart Scholars non-profit organization, along with three other powerful women. This scholarship is given out annually to African American females from her hometown of Wadesboro, North Carolina who are attending college to help with their expenses. Dr. Little believes it takes a village to raise a child and she also encourages others to never forget where you come from. Dr. Little is a strong believer in giving back to her community. She believes our young ladies need vision, direction and strong mentorship. She is the CEO/Founder/Visionary Author of The HBCU Experience Movement, LLC, the first Black-owned company to launch books written and published by prominent alumni throughout the world who attended Historically Black Colleges & Universities (HBCUs). As authors, they share a powerful collection of stories on how their unique college experience has molded them into the people they are today. The purpose of The HBCU Experience Movement is to change the narrative by sharing Black stories and investing financially back into our HBCUs to increase young alumni giving and enrollment. The award-winning bestselling authors won the Black Authors Matter TV Award in May of 2021, Inaugural Anthem Awards of 2022, as well as the International Book Awards by The American Book Fest. The books are also part of the WorldCat.org, the world's largest network of library content and services. Dr. Little is also the Editor and Chief of *Creating Your Seat at The Table International Magazine*, advisor for She Wins Society, and writing and publishing coach for the WILDE Winner's Circle.

She is the founder and owner of T.A.L.K. Radio & TV Network, LLC, which airs in over 167 countries, and streams live on Facebook, YouTube, Twitter and Periscope. This broadcasting and media production company is for new or existing radio shows, television shows, or other electronic media outlets to air content from a centralized source. All news, information or music shared on this platform are solely the responsibility of the station/radio owner. She is also the owner and creator of Creative Broadcasting Radio Station, the station of "unlimited possibilities." She is also one of the hosts of the new TV Show *Daytime Drama* nationally syndicated television show, which will be aired on Comcast Channel 19 and AT&T Channel 99 in 19 middle Tennessee counties. It will also air on The United Broadcasting Network, The Damascus Roads Broadcasting Network, and Roku.

Dr. Little is a 17X award-winning bestselling author of, *Dear Fear, Volume 2: 18 Powerful Lessons of Living Your Best Life Outside of Fear*; *The Gyrlfriend Code, Volume 1*; *I Survived; Girl, Get Up and Win*; *Glambitious Guide to Being an Entrepreneur*; *The Price of Greatness*; *The Making of a Successful Business Woman*; and *Hello, Queen*. She is a co-host for The Tamie Collins Markee Radio Show, award-winning entrepreneur who is also a reflection contributor for the book, NC Girls Living in a Maryland World, Sales/Marketing/ Contributing Writer/Event Correspondent for *SwagHer Magazine*, contributing writer for MizCEO Magazine, contributing editor for *SheIs Magazine*, contributing writer/national sales executive for *Courageous Woman Magazine*, contributing writer for Upwords International Magazine (India), and contributing writer/global partner for Powerhouse Global International Magazine(London). Host of "Creating Your Seat At The Table", Host of "Authors On The Rise", Co-Host Glambitious Podcast, Partner/Visionary Author of The Gyrlfriend Code The Sorority Edition along with The Gyrlfriend Collective, LLC. Lastly, she has received awards, such as "Author of the Month"; The Executive Citation of Anne Arundel County, Maryland Award, which was awarded by the County Executive Steuart L. Pittman; and Top 28 Influential Business Pioneers for *K.I.S.H. Magazine* Spring 2019 Edition. She has been featured in *All About Inspire Magazine, Formidable Magazine, BRAG Magazine,* the front cover of MizCEO Magazine in November of 2019, the front cover for Upwords Magazine in the October 2019 Edition, *Courageous Woman* Special Speakers Edition in November 2019 and *Influence Magazine.* She has been featured on a nationally syndicated television show, *HBCU 101,* on Aspire TV, Dynasty of Dreamers *K.I.S.H. Magazine* Spring 2019 Edition, the front cover of *Courageous Magazine* in December of 2019, the front cover of Doz International Magazine in January 2020, Top 28 Influential Business Pioneers for *K.I.S.H. Magazine, Power20 Magazine Glambitious* January 2020 and *Power20 Magazine Glambitious* February 2020. She was also featured in *Powerhouse Global International London Magazine* March 2020 edition, *National Boss Magazine* in the October 2020 edition, *Sheen Magazine* February 2020 edition as one of "The Top 20 Women to Be on The Lookout for in 2020", BlackNews.com, BlackBusiness.com, the front cover of *She Speaks Magazine* August 2020 edition, as well as the front cover of *National Boss Magazine* November 2020 edition.

In addition, she's been featured on BlackNewsScoop.com, awarded the National Women's Empowerment Ministry "Young, Gifted & Black Award" in February 2020, which honors and celebrates women in business below age 40 for their creativity and business development. Featured in *National Women Empowerment Magazine, Black Enterprise,* as well as on Fox, NBC, and CBS, she was interviewed on *The Black Report* on Fox Soul TV and the front cover for *National Boss Magazine.* She was also a speaker at The Black College Expo 2020, for Creative CEOs Summit in January of 2021, and international speaker for Living Your Dream Life Summit 2021. She was also the speaker for the Elite Business Women Powershift Conference 2021, The Bella, The Brand & Her Bag Wealth Summit 2021, The Unstoppable You Summit in January 2021, the Marketing Mastery Summit for Glambitious 2021, the Crown Yourself Conference in January 2021, as well as the Door Dash Virtual Black History Month Celebration. As the speaker for Day of Aggie Generations with North Carolina A&T State University, Dr. Little was the 2021 Woman of Black Excellence Honoree, guest speaker on the podcast, The Happy Hour Show, speaker for the Phoenix Jack & Jill HBCU Author Showcase, as well as a guest on The JMosley Show. As contributing author for *Prayers for The Entrepreneurial Woman* book, she has spoken at Creative Con, been recognized as one of Today's Black History Makers, as well as being a featured speaker at From Paper to Profits Conference. She has been afforded the opportunity to gain press access for "Don't Waste Your Petty" movie as well as Mahalia Jackson's movie. She's been a speaker for HerStory Women's Global Empowerment Summit, HerStory Women Who Lead Conference, Stepping N2 Sisterhood Sharing Winning Secrets Virtual Summit, I AM Glambitious Virtual Conference, Black Authors Matter TV show, Thought Leaders Global Virtual Summit, as well as A Conversation with Floyd Marshall, Jr. As a Black Authors Matter TV award winner, she has spoken for Sheen Talk and served as the foreword author for the anthology *It Cost to Be the Boss.* Recognized by *VIP Global Magazine* as one of the Top 50 Most Influential Women, she has spoken at Black Writers Weekend, The GameChangers with Angela Ward Show, and served as keynote speaker for Blacks in Nonprofits Conference. Having served as speaker for the Leap

Conference, Pass the Mic Sis, the From Purpose to Profit Summit, and The Been Worthy Podcast, she has been the speaker and host for The MizCEO graduation, was featured in *Emoir Magazine* for Building a Global Media Empire, and was a Making Black History Today recipient for Glambitious.

Dr. Little received her undergraduate degree in English from North Carolina A&T State University. She received her master's degree in Industrial Organizational Psychology and her Doctorate in Leadership, as well. Dr. Little is a mover and shaker, and she continuously pushes herself to be better than she was yesterday. She gives God all the credit for everything that has happened in her life. She has strong faith and determination to be great. She believes her only competition is herself. Her favorite scripture is Philippians 4:13: "I can do all things through Christ who strengthens me."

# Table of Contents



*continued...*

# DR. RODERICK LITTLE

# Foreword
## Reaping True Support for What We Love
### Dr. Roderick Little
### Director of Bands, Jackson State University

For decades, HBCU band programs have been systematically connected and embedded in not only the HBCU higher education environment but also the African American community. African American culture has also been very instrumental in reshaping and imagining almost every aspect of our civilization from how our environments are built, what we eat, and how we dress, to music. We've added our unique touch of perspective and culture that adds a more profound sense of entertainment value, feeling, and soul which is captivating for ethnicities. Culturally, our food is seasoned differently making it a bit more flavorful, our style of dress is more striking that can express one's personality, and our music evokes feelings through our unique blend of textures and harmonies that cannot be recreated. Because all of these attributes are directly correlated to who we are as an ethnicity, it's directly connected to our ethnic identity. As a result, all things that are "culturally" connected to us, have an historic relevance and value that is highly supported and protected.

Our bands have taken on an identity and space of their own. Historically, the initial role of the bands was to provide support for the football teams and add to the overall gameday experience. As mentioned prior, our HBCU band programs have since then morphed to much more. From just clean marching company fronts on the field, while playing a standard march to playing popular music and incorporating dance routines, these are a few attributes that have changed the face of the HBCU band. Because of the implementation of showmanship and entertainment, HBCU bands are now seen as a separate entity of the football experience. Not to take away from our football teams in the HBCU space because they are indeed a very vital part to our institutions but you will often hear fans say that they come to the games just to see the bands. In the HBCU space, even if the football team may be having an unsuccessful season, attendance will still be representative just to see the bands.

For decades now, bands can easily run their own events affectionately known as "Battle of the Bands" and gain a high level of interest, to say the least. The HBCU band culture even has an outgrowth of these events through summer bands. Depending on the event, a stadium of 50,000 people can be full to capacity just to see the bands. There are no other extracurricular activities outside of sports that can draw this kind of crowd; this includes PWI band programs as well. In addition to this, because of the energy that our programs exude, major corporations, television stations, promoters, etc. have taken notice and often request bands to be a part of parades, reality tv shows, commercials, and the list goes on and on. Again, to reiterate, this is not the case for other programs outside of the HBCU space.

This type of notoriety is special and most definitely not taken for granted because the talents of our students are showcased on a national level. Although the notoriety is appreciated, there is a problem that we have encountered. With all the eyes and grandeur of our programs, you'd think that all of the opportunities would bring financial stability to our programs however, it is the polar opposite. Unfortunately, historically, it has been the case for our (African American) intellectual property and talents to be exploited and not be adequately funded but rather to make a profit for other entities. There is no question that people understand the importance of HBCU programs however, the understanding does not equate to financial support. It is no secret that HBCUs are underfunded and we often have to fund ourselves internally, however, because our bands receive so much attention, the question is, why aren't our programs funded properly for our students' time, talent and our programs name image, and likeness. The events or opportunities we perform for can clear millions of dollars however, our programs are left with not even a percentage of that when we are the face of promotion and marketing.

It is important to reiterate that the attention and appreciation for our programs is a privilege understanding that it is not afforded to all however, we must speak up for ourselves and assert our importance and have our programs financially supported as such. Because our programs mean so much to not just our institutions but to our nation; it's no better time than this for those that request our presence to perform on national scales to either create endowments for our programs, secure sponsors and donors, or provide consistent donations so we can continue to foster, grow and support these programs that bring so much enjoyment to televisions, stadiums, and streets that we perform. People put their money where they really support- hopefully, this would start positive conversations to provide longevity and substantial financial stability for our programs. This wonderful book, and all its volumes, further substantiates the overwhelming evidence of the importance of truly supporting our programs.

## About Dr. Roderick Little

Dr. Roderick Little currently serves as Director of Bands/Assistant Professor of Music at Jackson State University. He received his Bachelors and Masters in Music Education, and a Doctorate in Urban Higher Education Administration, all from Jackson State University. A native of Jackson, MS, he grew up in a musical family/background. During his matriculation at JSU he participated in several ensembles including the famous "Sonic Boom of the South" where he played in the percussion section as a snare drummer, marched as part of the Jackson Five Drummajor squad, and also served as a student arranger for the Sonic Boom and student conductor of the Symphonic Band. Dr. Little studied percussion under Dr. Owen Rockwell, whom is his predecessor at JSU. After completing his undergraduate studies, he returned to his high school alma mater, Lanier High School. During his tenure at Lanier, his bands received excellent and superior ratings at marching/concert festivals. He also had students that made the Mississippi All State Lions Band (top student honor band in MS).

In 2012, Dr. Little began as Assistant Band Director and Instructor of Music at Jackson State University. He was promoted to Associate Director of Bands in 2013 and later, Marching Band Director in 2015. While Director of the Marching Band, he has maintained the rich traditions of the Sonic Boom while adding a unique twist with the use of technology and other innovative ideas. As director, Dr. Little started several outreach programs which include, but are not limited to, the Summer High School Band Camp and A Day With the Boom; both which act as major recruitment agents for the Department of Music/band program grossing over 400-600 students collectively annually. He started the public media relations of the Sonic Boom with the implementation of the Sonic Boom Media Team and strengthened social media platforms. Most importantly, he improved the inner workings of the overall operations of the entire JSU Band(s) program.

As the drill writer for the Sonic Boom of the South having had several monumental field shows adding to the bands lustrous history of band pageantry, In the spring of 2020, the Sonic Boom of the South's "Saints Halftime Show- Salute to the Veterans" was selected to be featured at the CBDNA-NBC Southern Division Conference which was the first appearance in the schools history.  He also arranged a massive catalog of music for the Sonic Boom of the South.  His other duties at Jackson State include co-conductor of the wind ensemble, conductor of the symphonic band, director of percussion ensemble and teaching in the percussion studio. He has acquired several new percussion instruments through NASM upgrades (an initiative started by Dr. Owen Rockwell and Dr. Darcie Bishop), which include steel pans for the percussion studio. Dr. Little also assists with observing student teachers during their clinical teaching experience(s) and has motivated several students to become successful teachers and performers. His research interest is centered on strengthening music education in urban at-risk areas.

Dr. Little is an accomplished conductor, clinician, adjudicator, composer, arranger, drill writer, and instrumentalist.  He has served as a guest clinician in numerous states across the country including Mississippi, Tennessee, Georgia, Louisiana and California.  He has arranged for numerous middle and high schools, colleges, chamber groups, jazz ensembles and church conventions. He has also scored piano music for F & S Music KC Publishing Company, which was founded by Lannie Spann McBride, a former instructor of music at JSU and revered church musician and keen motivator.  He performed with local groups around Jackson, MS and momentarily in Houston, TX. He has professional affiliations with The National Association for Music Education (NAfME), Percussive Art Society (PAS), Mississippi Association of Education (MAE), Mississippi Band Masters Association (MBA), HBCU National Band Directors

Consortium (HBCU-NBDC) and College Band Directors National Association (CBDNA).

He is married to Lynise Little whom he met at JSU in the "Sonic Boom." They were the first to do a joint recital at Jackson State showcasing the music of both classical and contemporary jazz genres. They have two sons, Aiden and Alec Little.

# SHONNIE MURRELL

# Foreword
# The "BEST BAND IN THE UNIVERSE"
## Shonnie Murrell
## Grambling State University

Historically Black College and University Marching Bands have been around since 1890. We are the heartbeat of every school and without us there would not be enough excitement. You can hear the drum majors whistle blowing, the drums striking, and the instrumentation playing from miles away.

In 1926, the most world-renowned band in history the "World Famed" Tiger marching band was created by Ralph Waldo Emerson and in 1952 the legend Conrad Hutchinson Jr. came in and implemented our marching styles, drills, precision, cadences, uniforms and so much more.

When I attended Alma J. Brown Elementary located on Grambling State University campus, I remember seeing that band marching, dancers dancing and the drum majors were the ones who caught my eyes. As a little kid looking at this amazing band, I remember being extremely excited!

So, every time after I would get out of school, I would have to go to my mother's beauty salon LaWAnda's Hair Care Center, by the bus station in Grambling. I knew that my baby-sitter, as I would call her Molly, who is a die-hard alumni, would take me on the yard. I would have the time of my life because she has always been known as the "Life of the Party." My dad Fredrick who later became the President of Douglas L. Williams Alumni Chapter, he would also take me around the yard to experience everything as well.

Most of my relatives attended Grambling and just HBCUs in general so the culture was instilled in me at a young age. Just imagine a real life "Different World" but in reality, being a part of black excellence was a must.

The World Famed is known across the entire world literally! This historic band has traveled around the world to places such as Africa, Japan, Korea, Bahamas, Cuba, Philippines, and Panama to name a few. This historic band has performed at multiple presidential inaugurations and in major television commercials, television appearances, movies, reality television and so much more!

One day the legendary Dr. Edwin Thomas of the World Famed Tiger Marching band came to Jack Yates high school to audition students. I was sweating bullets the entire time! He had a straight face the whole time. I ended up being a P1 which meant I gained a full scholarship.

My band directors were amazing Dr. Larry Pannell as the head band director and the all-star staff: Dr. Edwin Thomas, Mr. Charles Lacy, Mr. Malcom Spencer and Ms. Cowan.

All of them are characters, as I like to call them the barbershop characters from "Coming to America." It was never a dull moment with them. In the words of Dr. Pannell, "Nothing comes to a sleeper but a dreamer, so while you're out here sleeping someone is living your dream!" I can hear him yelling this across the field and band room still to this day!

As an incoming freshman, I knew that it would be hard work, dedication and that my life was about to change forever. On August 1st, all band personnel had to report to campus together for the 2nd time in the band's history, so that by itself was somewhat intimidating. Usually, the freshmen arrive the first week of August and the second week the upperclassmen arrive. Being that our first football game was in San Jose, CA as a freshman we only had two weeks to learn everything, but I had to learn additional things being that I was on the Drumline.

Every morning our drill sergeants would make sure that we were out on the pavement at 5:00 am not a minute or second late. We would march from our temporary dormitory to the band hall "Dunbar," where we would have March from 8 to 5 on the lines as well as dots painted out. And to think that we would have a little break, the "devil" himself as we called him, would be standing waiting for our arrival! His name is Terry Lily, the cheerleader coach / fitness trainer legend! If you were out of shape when your parents dropped you off at school by the time Terry Lily finished with you, your parents would not recognize who you were when they saw you doing football season!

And to think it would stop there, the United States Marine Corp would train us next with running exercises, more fitness training and drilling. I can still hear that military sergeant yell out "Eyeballs" and we would have to respond with "Snap", a command given to look at him while standing at attention without turning your head.

My father James aka "Spike" who is not only a U.S. Marine veteran, Marine boxing Hall-Famer, first African- American Chief of Police and now Mayor of Jonesboro, Louisiana instilled in me the many things that he learned while in the Marines. So, unlike a few of my crab brothers and sisters I could adjust quite well.

Now the actual marching drilling begins, then off to breakfast we go in which student leaders made sure we were only drinking water! Our water intake was over eight glasses at times but we needed it especially due to the humid heat.

It is no walk in the park and as I remember I called my dad Fredrick to tell him to come pick me up one night! He told me to go harder and show them what I had to offer as well as to remember who it is that I am. When he told me that, that is just what I did! I went so hard that no one could stop me.

Being the only freshman female on not one drum but four at one time had not ever been done by a female in the World Famed. I am honored to say that I am the first female quad/quint player, Freshman of the Year, and Drill Sergeant to the highest position as the Master Drill Sergeant.

Going hard was first nature to me, no one could tell me that I could not achieve anything! I am not only going to show you, but I made sure that I added extra punches for you to feel.

In my era of the band, we were in The Great Debaters as well as multiple ESPN commercials, NBA half-time shows, NFL half-time shows, reality shows, and parades. Speaking of parades, the one that sticks out the most for me is the Rose Bowl parade in which we were honored by George Lucas himself to be named the best Band of the Universe! We were in Star Wars costumes, we had customized STAR WARS drumheads with our World Famed logos and more! People went crazy when they saw and heard us!

Being a personality on our reality show "Season of the Tiger" was a great experience in which many people still to this day, tell me that they attended an HBCU because they watched the show. This show opened many doors for me and the relationships that were built are because of the World Famed.

As a former Director of Fine Arts, I have instilled in my students to be a part of something great and to go hard no matter what is thrown their way. My little brother is heading to Grambling to be a part of the World Famed as I have told him, he is legacy all the way around and it is his time to shine! He will be amazing in the World Famed trombone section, and he also has the stature of a drum major!

That uniform is like putting on a superman or woman uniform and you are recognized by the entire world, standing on the shoulders of the ones before you and you have no choice but to feel the Tiger Pride!

My HBCU Marching Band taught me that nothing is given to you, it is earned, be the very best that you can be and remember that "G" always and will forever stand for GREATNESS!

## About Shonnie Murrell

Known by her stage name "Shonnie Murrell", LaShonda Antrionette Harris was born on July 19 in Jonesboro, Louisiana and raised in Houston, Texas. She has been singing and playing instruments since the age of 3.

Shonnie graduated from Sharpstown High School and received a Bachelor of Science degree in Business Management from Grambling State University. Shonnie can contribute her showmanship on percussion to her years she spent marching in the Grambling State World Famed Tiger Marching band. She is not only the first female to play Quads & Quints but she also held the highest position in the band as Master Drill Sgt. and was one of the main reality personalities on the hit BET show *"Season of the Tiger"*. From this she landed a spot on *106 and Park*, BET awards and other television appearances.

She is also a part of the Class of 2022 RECORDING ACADEMY (GRAMMYS) in which she sits on the education committee.

Funk Potion #9, which she names when performing with her full rhythm section and band, loves to give her fans the greatest performance on earth. Shonnie believes that her energy and engaging the audience are two key elements that are important to accomplish this feat! She is most of the time compared to Sheila E., Erykah Badu, and Missy Elliot because of her ability to mix her sound, lyrical, 2nd-Line, GOGO music and visual poetry all together.

Some notables that Shonnie has performed with or opened for include:

Most recent, Percussionist for CholexHalle & Uche from *American Idol* at Houston Mayors Spectacular Event, Performer for Dikembe Mutumbo Congo Foundation.

Performer for Freedom Over Texas, headliner for Austin Crawfish Fest, headliner for San Antonio, TX Mardi Gras, KPC Convention, Seer Seekers & Sundresses in Atlanta, GA.

National Anthem Singer for Rockets vs Spurs, Pelicans vs Thunder.

Cameo *Real Housewives of Atlanta*, Percussionist for Legendary group SWITCH. opening act for LEELA JAMES, MAJOR., RICK ROSS, LIL WAYNE. MC LYTE, WARREN G., MACSHAWN100, LETOYA LUCKETT, ERIC ROBERSON, YOUNG JOC, the late great AL JARREAU and FRANK MCCOMB, to name a few. Her performances have taken her all over the world!

Shonnie Murrell also helps Title 1 schools (12 schools to be exact) upstart their Fine Arts programs along with her partnership with Microsoft.

# DR. CHRISTY A. WALKER

# Bandhead for Life

**Dr. Christy A. Walker**

**North Carolina A&T State University**

I guess I was destined to be a member of an HBCU band. It's literally in my blood.

My earliest memory of seeing a HBCU marching band was when I was about four years old. Both of my parents were graduates of North Carolina A&T, where they met in the band. They were loyal alumni and attended A&T football games every season. When they brought me to games, I never paid attention to the football game itself, but the music always kept my attention.

I grew up in Hampton, Virginia, a city in close proximity to not one, but two HBCUs:  Hampton Institute (now University), in Hampton, and Norfolk State University, which was thirty minutes away in Norfolk. I can recall attending Hampton football games at Armstrong Stadium with my grandmother when I was around five years old. Again, my eyes glazed over during the football game. However, I was always excited to see the band and the halftime show. I'll never forget those halftime band battles between Hampton and Norfolk State, known as the "Battle of the Bay", in the early 80's. Even as a five-year-old, I could tell that that band battle was intense! I knew that when I grew up, I would be in a band just like that.

I first met "Prof" Walter Carlson, A&T's band director when my parents marched, when I was six years old. He happened to be in town one day and stopped by our house to visit. Growing up, I always heard stories of how my parents marched at A&T under Prof. Carlson, how my dad was band president and trombone section leader, and how my mom was band secretary, a music major, and the only female member of A&T's brass ensemble.

By the time I reached high school, I knew I wanted to march at A&T. I had watched A&T's band every year for a decade. I knew I wanted to be there. Contrary to popular belief, my parents never forced me to go to A&T. They did, however, tell me they would pay for college if I attended an HBCU. It was *that* important to them. Regardless of influence, I had good grades, and I learned to play clarinet (my main instrument), flute, and piano. I was section leader in my high school band, and I played in all-city and regional bands.

I attended A&T's Visitors' Day for prospective students during my senior year, and met A&T's band director, Dr. Johnny B. Hodge, better known as "Doc", at the football game. I was nervous at first, but I walked up to Doc and introduced myself as Chauncey and Zenobia's daughter. He smiled, put his hand on my shoulder, pointed to the band and said, "Next year, you will be here." That was reassuring to hear.

The summer before my first band camp was a whirlwind. I was looking forward to marching in A&T's band, known as the "Blue and Gold Marching Machine". I knew there would be a big difference in my high school marching band experience and my college experience. My high school marched "corps style"—a roll step march with our feet close to the ground. I knew that A&T (and all other HBCU bands) primarily marched with a high-step style, which was much more physically demanding. I knew this would be a big adjustment, and I tried to get in physical shape ahead of time by running in my neighborhood in the combat boots I purchased for camp.

Our band camp schedule was as follows:

- 4:15 a.m. – Wake up (clothes were laid out the night before), shower, dress, walk to the practice field.

- 5 a.m. to 7 a.m. – Marching rehearsal

- 7 a.m. to– 9 a.m. – Breakfast and a quick nap

- 9 a.m.  to 11 a.m. – Indoor music rehearsal

- 11 a.m. to 1 p.m. – Lunch

- 1 p.m. to 3 p.m. – Another music rehearsal

- 3 p.m. to 5 p.m. – Dinner

- 5 p.m. until – Outdoor rehearsal and sectionals

We did this all in the August heat. By September, I was in the best shape of my life.

I ended up marching for A&T all four years of college. We faced quite a few bands during those four years, but there are three memorable battles I would like to focus on:

The first collegiate game I played in was against Winston-Salem State University (WSSU) in September. I will always remember the exact day of this game because it was my eighteenth birthday! WSSU was only thirty minutes away from A&T and was historically one of A&T's biggest rivals. My mother grew up in Winston-Salem. Two of my aunts graduated from WSSU, and another aunt worked on the WSSU campus. That game was more than a rivalry – it was a family reunion.

Marching in that first game was intimidating. I knew the music, the formations and the dance routine. I had practiced it dozens of times, but it wasn't the same thing as actually performing it in front of a full crowd in Winston-Salem. All I kept thinking throughout the performance was, *Don't mess up! Don't forget to turn at the right time! Don't forget the dance routine and don't fall!* But all was well. The halftime show went on without issues.

The Winston-Salem game was also the first game where I faced an opposing band. I loved the feeling of literally facing your opponent and blowing songs in their direction. Then, of course, after the game, both bands played songs back and forth at each other, better known as a "5th Quarter".

The second game that was significant to me as a bandsman was the 1994 Circle City Classic in Indianapolis, when A&T played Southern University. Southern's band had a great reputation. I had grown up seeing their halftime show every year on NBC when they played Grambling State in the Bayou Classic. I was excited to see them face to face.

Southern's band had been known to intimidate other bands due to their powerful sound and overall swagger. But they didn't intimidate us! I am glad that Doc taught us never to be intimidated by another band. That lesson sticks with me to this day. Back then, the Machine's nickname was the "Small Band with the Big Sound". We weren't really *that* small, but we were smaller than Southern's band. However, we didn't *sound* small. We ended up winning the Battle of the Bands that year. And, yes, we won because we received a trophy engraved with us as the winners, which is probably in A&T's band room somewhere.

The third game was when we played FAMU in 1996, my last year marching. It was significant because the band traveled to Tallahassee, Florida for the game. All of us recognized the history and legacy of Florida A&M's Marching 100. Bragg Stadium, FAMU's stadium, had a reputation of being tough to play in. FAMU's fan base is strong, and their fans are really passionate about their school. Not many bands traveled there.

Once again, the Blue and Gold Marching Machine was *not* intimidated by FAMU's band (or any others). Doc gave us the spirit of, "I'm not scared of anybody!", and it showed. We went in and played during the game and the halftime show, just as if we were in Aggie Stadium. At the end of the game, we filed out of our seats and walked across the field. We set up in concert formation in front of where FAMU was sitting. From there, our band and FAMU's band played songs back and forth during a "5th Quarter".

I don't remember who started it first, but both bands ended up playing some songs together. There was a rare spirit of camaraderie between the two HBCU bands. That night, FAMU's band threw a party and invited us. I still laugh about that party when I talk to people who were in FAMU's band back then.

When I think back to my time in the Blue and Gold Marching Machine, I have fond memories. I know people say that they met their best friends or their spouse through the band. People may be surprised, though, to find out that my best friends were not *necessarily* people I marched with in the band. Regardless, I still took away many lessons from the band. I learned musicianship, discipline, consistency, goal setting and, most importantly, confidence.

Now that I work as a college administrator, I have learned to appreciate the cultural significance of HBCU bands. I've learned to appreciate how they help in increasing student morale, refining campus culture, and bringing publicity to the university. They are the face of the university. They are the heart of HBCUs.

After college, I continued to keep up with HBCU band culture. In 1999, along with Michael Lee, I established an online community for HBCU bands called the 5th Quarter. Through The 5th Quarter, I have had the chance to mingle with people from just about every HBCU band. I've hosted gatherings, sat in luxury suites at stadiums, and even went on a cruise. However, I am proudest of the fact that, through my website, I was able to encourage students to march in an HBCU band.

The HBCU band family is a family. We have our quirks like any other family. But what I love the most is that I could meet anybody who marched in an HBCU band and have a common experience to talk about. It's been over 35 years since I started following HBCU bands. I used to think that I would never be that person in their 40s following HBCU bands. Now that I am in my 40s, I don't know what I was thinking back then. I have finally faced the fact that I'm gonna be a bandhead for life.

# About Dr. Christy A. Walker

Dr. Christy A. Walker, is a higher education professional, career counselor, and HBCU advocate.

Christy, a native of Hampton, Virginia, earned a bachelor's degree in Chemical Engineering from North Carolina Agricultural and Technical State University. While Christy was a student at A&T, she was a member of the Blue and Gold Marching Machine. She was also active in the American Institute of Chemical Engineers (AIChE) and the National Society of Black Engineers (NSBE).

Christy's first roles after A&T were as an environmental chemist and as an engineer. Christy eventually transitioned to the education field and earned a master's degree in Higher Education Administration from Old Dominion University. She most recently earned a doctorate in Higher Education Administration from Northeastern University. She currently serves as a Career Program Director at Tech Elevator after a 20+ year career in higher education.

In 1999, Christy, along with Michael Lee, created The 5th Quarter, a website dedicated to showcasing HBCU marching bands. The 5th Quarter was considered a top resource for HBCU marching bands and received tens of thousands of unique visitors annually until its closing in 2019, after 20 years of service. The 5th Quarter has been profiled on the Huffington Post, and Christy has been interviewed on HBCU bands by the *New York Times*, CNN, the Associated Press, *HBCU Digest*, and the *Charlotte Post*.

Christy is also the creator of the podcast, The HBCU Band Experience with Christy Walker, in which Christy interviews marching band alumni from different HBCUs. She is an Honorary member the National Chapter of Tau Beta Sigma National Honorary

Band Sorority and a member of Sigma Alpha Iota International Music Fraternity.

Christy is the Lead Author in *The HBCU Experience: HBCU Band Alumni Edition Volumes 1* and *2*, which brought 70 alumni members of HBCU bands together to share their experiences.

# JOHN "SKIP" WILSON

# THE BOX
## THE PV MACFUNK BOX 1989
### The Rise of the Drum Feature

**John "SKIP" Wilson**

**The Prairie View A&M University Drumline**

August in all bandheads lives is filled with an excited anxious energy. "Why?", you ask. It's because we knew that soon, band camp was about to start. Band camp was more exciting to us than all of the Classic football games and homecoming rolled into one. Band camp is when all of your close friends come back to school, the music starts, and in my case, the drums get to drumming. There's a high anticipation about what level your band was going to be on for the upcoming year, how big or small that the band was going to be, how the band was going to look, and how the band was going to sound. Truth be told, we couldn't wait to get back to the partying, the girls, and the hanging out, because in my world, Prairie View A&M University was the place to be.

Now, there's one element of band camp that I didn't talk about yet, and that's "the Crabs." Crabs are what we oldheads or upper-class band members affectionately call freshmen band members. Every year, you have your hyped crabs, your lazy crabs, your arrogant crabs, your babied crabs, the crabs that have never been away from home crabs, and your sheltered crabs. It was our job to figure out who was who so that we could start molding them into band members that we would eventually call brothers and sisters. We also knew that every crab that came to band camp wouldn't make it to the end of band camp, because band camp was designed to filter out the worthy from the unworthy, the strong from the weak, and to find out who had heart or not. Band camp was hard on us, so we knew that it was going to be twice as hard on them because all of us oldheads were once crabs.  But when band camp started, we knew that it was band season, and when it is band season, it's time for war, so let the music begin.

The year is 1989, and this is the year that the drum world was flipped upside down.  Our band director, Professor George "Prof Ed" Edwards was on a mission, he was literally trying to build the best HBCU band in America.  He was always innovating, always perfecting and always trying to be better than every other band around.  Prof Ed had only been the head band director for five years. He became the head band director in 1984 with seventy-five band members, I crabbed in 1987 and we ballooned to about one hundred and eighty band members. We were known for a great halftime show with an up-tempo drill, and an unbelievable concert tune arranged by him and sung by Teri Ellis before she became a member of world renown music group En Vogue and Ricky LaFontaine before he was a member of the gospel choir The Richard Smallwood Singers.  We also had a high energy dance routine composed of the latest dance music, a high energy dance, and the straightest lines for that extra element of perfection.

This year, Prof Ed wanted more, he in his gut felt like there was a piece of the puzzle that was missing, he called it the drum feature. A drum feature is a halftime show inside of a halftime show that highlights the playing skills of our drumline better known as the PV MACFUNK BOX or THE BOX for short.

It was either day two or day three of band camp and Prof came to us and said that he wanted to feature the BOX at halftime.  We were like "what?"  He said that he wanted the BOX to do a halftime show inside of the halftime show, and we laughed and got excited because we were already cocky and wanted to battle any and everybody at anytime, anywhere.  At this point in time, Joe Jackson and Rodney Goods were our section leaders and they were music majors and seriously deep into their craft, so this was right up their alley. So that night, they started writing the foundation to what would be the first feature named "The Fuege." Joe and Rodney came to practice a couple of days later and presented to us an unfinished masterpiece, and we read it and played it, and before they could finish it, The Fuege took on a life of its own. Here's the thing, we had a very talented bunch of young men and women that could really play drums, so taking their concept and elaborating on it was easy only because we were so creative and understood where we were going with it.

Now that we had a semi-finished cadence, we had to incorporate it into the band somehow. We had to figure out where to put it and how to merge it and then it happened, synergy. We figured it out and Prof loved it. The feature had the high energy, the crowd appeal, and the flash that Prof was looking for, his vision was now a reality, the Drum Feature was born. The first time that we performed the feature was in Dallas at the State Fair Classic. This game was against one of our biggest rivals, the Grambling State Tigers. Their drumline was named Chocolate Thunder. This game always had a crowd size of at least sixty-five thousand fans and it was packed. This game was always a big game and it seemed like all of the Black people in Dallas came to this game. Most of the student body from both schools would definitely be there and the alumni from Prairie View and Grambling would converge on the Cotton Bowl for this game from all over the world. The energy was high and the stadium had no idea about what was about to happen. Then all of a sudden, it was HALFTIME, and the crowd went crazy, and it was a success. They just witnessed the birth of the drum feature and Prof Ed was happy beyond belief.

As the years progressed and as the features got more creative and more advanced, we took them to more aggressive heights. We started doing acrobatics, throwing drums to each other, throwing sticks and mallets to each other from ten yards away, crawling through each other's legs, climbing on shoulders, playing upside down and we added cymbal twirls that were amazing. The BOX was doing routines that were more advanced and more mesmerizing than any other drumline in the world. We had a cult following that was so large that every city that we went to, we were amazed to see that all of the drumlines were playing our drum cadences and trying to mimic our moves, it was amazing. Looking back, I am realizing that we had a large finger print and this much social impact, before Myspace, YouTube, Facebook, Twitter and Instagram. We had people recording us with the giant VHS camcorders and the little hand-held recorders, and these people would share these tapes amongst themselves. I'm just happy that a lot of people had the wherewithal to dig into their old dusty boxes and upload the videos to YouTube and now we have a resurgence of the excitement that we brought.

Over the years, I started to see more and more HBCU drumlines use our style of drumming, and incorporated it into their own styles. We created what is now known as Show Style drumming and I love to see it. The Prairie View MacFunk BOX started as a "funk" drumline, then we incorporated a more technical style of playing and we coined it as "TechnoFunk." The BOX went on to dominate the HBCU DrumWorld for the next three decades and we continue to be the most relevant drumline in the twenty-first century.

Professor George "Prof Ed" Edwards unfortunately died on May 28, 2009 from complications due to a car wreck in Houston, Texas and he is buried not far from the band room where he made magic happen. Prof Ed is truly missed and would be proud to see that his legacy is alive and well. The Prairie View A&M University Marching Band is known as the Marching Storm and we continue to still wow the crowds and win awards everywhere that we perform. When we hit the field and spell the letters P.V.U. and play our traditional introduction song Entertainment Tonight, my pride level goes to one hundred and I always think of Prof Ed at that moment. I always remember his hard work and all that he did to create a dynasty. I miss his words of wisdom, his guidance, and definitely his fussing. Rest well Prof Edwards, you touched so many lives and so many souls.  You are truly missed, and you are truly loved, you will never be forgotten.

Here is a link, this link is a mix of the first Feature in 1989 until about 1996 I hope that you enjoy it, https://youtu.be/V69rIiVV09w. Oh yeah just listen to the crowds.

*REST WELL TO ALL OF THE BOX SOLDIERS THAT DIED KNOWING THAT THEY LEFT THEIR FINGERPRINTS ON A LEGACY AND A DYNASTY.  B.O. B.O.*

# About John "SKIP" Wilson

John "SKIP" Wilson is a native Houstonian that fell in love with drums at an early age.  It all started by him taking the pots and pans out of the cabinets and driving his mother crazy by constantly beating and beating while she was trying to cook.  One day a friend of his that lived five houses down from him, his mother, threw away his Muppet's drum set. He saw it and he asked her if he could have it and she said yes.  SKIP was nine years old and this ironically was the start of a lifelong love of playing drums.  Although that toy drum set didn't last but about two weeks, his love and passion flourished. The very next year, he was in the 6th grade and God gave him a band class and the band director, Mr. Hurdle let him choose the drums and he excelled.  He later attended Kashmere Senior High School and the band director Mr. LeBlanc encouraged and demanded creativity so that's what we did, created.  At Kashmere there were four brothers, the Taylor Boys Ricky, Pat, Mack, and Terry, that had all the style and pizazz that made for a pitri dish of creativity, style, love, and showmanship. We had a very good drumline. Then in 1987 Mr. Wilson graduated and once again, God intervened, he enrolled at Prairie View A&M University and Majored in Psychology and Minored in English and this is where he met Professor George "Prof" Edwards and he "crabbed" (became a freshman member) In the greatest HBCU Band in the world.  The drumline at Prairie View was called The PV McFunk BOX, "THE BOX" for short and they were the next level of playing and performing with a drum, he knew that he was home.  He excelled, his drum skills and his creativity exploded and he helped create a style of drumming called "SHOWSTYLE".  When his years of service to The BOX as far as performing was at its end, Prof. Edwards made him the Assistant Percussion instructor assisting Professor Larry Jones with The BOX.  This relationship lasted until May of 2009 when unfortunately Professor Edwards died from complications due to a car wreck. In 2003 SKIP founded the Prairie View "Marching Storm" Band Alumni Association geared towards bridging the gap between the different eras of the band from the 1960's through the 2000's and raising much needed money that the band needed for equipment and scholarships.  He has volunteered and taught at several at-risk High Schools in the Houston area and helped facilitate scholarships to multiple colleges and universities. Some of those schools are Madison High School 98-99, Thurgood Marshall High School 2002-2006, North Forest High School 2009-to present, Alto Senior High School 2015 to present and he also consults and teaches at Forest Brook Middle School which is the feeder school to North Forest High School.  This has been a journey and he will do it as long as God wants him to.

# DR. BRIDGETTE CRAWFORD BELL

# The Orange and Blue Crush, MSU
## Dr. Bridgette Crawford Bell
### Morgan State University

I am Bridgette Crawford Bell, a proud alumnus of Morgan State University. The decision to attend college and participate in marching band is one that I did not take likely. The love for all things college football and band was instilled in me from childhood. My dad played football and was in the band while in high school in Alabama. I grew up watching Alabama State, Alabama A&M, Tuskegee, Morgan State, Auburn and, of course, The University of Alabama. On Saturdays, we spent our time watching college football and marching bands.

Our family is originally from a small town in Alabama; however, I grew up in Baltimore. My childhood home, located in northeast Baltimore, was less than five miles from Morgan State University. I cannot truly tell my story without connecting it to my family history. My dad is a Bishop, and for many years, he was the primary organist for our congregations. I loved music since I was a child and wanted to follow in my dad's footsteps.

From the age of eight years old, I learned the piano and the clarinet. During weekdays, my dad drove to the campus of Morgan State University to watch the football team and band practice. To us, watching the band rehearse was just as important as watching the football team practice. We would then leave Morgan, go home, and play marching band around the house. My dad would tap out the Morgan cadence while I marched behind him yelling, "Ayyy Oooo MSU!" This very thing instilled a love in me for the HBCU band culture.

In the 90s, not many HBCU bands received television coverage. The only bands to receive national television exposure were Southern and Grambling at The Bayou Classic. As a high school tuba student,

I knew that I wanted to attend an HBCU and major in Music. By senior year, I narrowed my choices down to my number one choice, Grambling. My second choice was Alabama State, and third choice was Morgan. It's safe to say that almost every child wants to move away for college. I was accepted into all three colleges, but soon narrowed my choices down to two. To my surprise, my top two choices were paired to play in a football classic during my senior year. The classic was held at the Old Memorial Stadium in Baltimore on September 17, 1994. I was even more excited about the battle of the bands set to happen the Friday night before the game.

As a senior, I was super excited. I knew this game would be my deciding factor. The day of the Battle of the Bands, I remember excitedly riding to Rash Field to watch. The announcer began as Morgan State Band marched onto the field. To my surprise, this normally small band had a nice boost in numbers. The Morgan State Band's energy was high, and they sounded good.

During the battle of the bands, Morgan played a few stand tunes and completed a field show. The crowd wondered when the guest band would arrive. To our dismay, the guest band never showed up. The next day, I arrived at Memorial Stadium early. I wanted to get an opportunity to meet the other band director. I approached him as the band warmed up, and he assured me that he would be visiting my high school. As I went to find my seat, I could hear an electric familiar sound coming through the tunnel. The Magnificent Marching Machine was chanting, "Ayyyyyy Ooo M-S-U!" with a fire that I'd never heard before. Everyone in the area went scrambling to find the sound. This band was hyped and electrifying.

The Morgan State Band was the smaller band. However, on that day, they packed a mighty punch. I clearly remember watching the much larger guest band take the field. They did their standard dance show. The Morgan State University Magnificent Marching Machine took the field and performed what I now know to be the "L" drill. The quality difference was clear. But if I needed more convincing, their stand performance was superior. The sound of "M3" playing Follow Me is clearly branded in my brain until this very day. I was totally sold, but I wanted to still give the other director the benefit of the doubt.

I was prepared to still audition for the band that I considered to be my number one choice. On Monday, September 19, the band director arrived at my high school. He was surprised to see an all-girl, predominately Black show-style band program. As he interviewed me, I explained that I was a tuba player. He gave me a serious side-glance and said, "A little thing like you playing the tuba? How about you try something else if you want to come to my school?"

I said, "No, sir. I am a tuba player."

He said, "You know our tubas are about sixty pounds. Do you think you can handle that?" I proceeded to sit down with my concert tuba and asked if we could continue the audition. I auditioned, but I knew I would no longer pursue that school. After my audition, he was astonished and proceeded to offer me a scholarship. However, I knew Morgan State University was going to be the place for me.

A few months later, Morgan State University invited me to their Fine Arts Day. The faculty performed, the ensembles performed, and I met with the band director. Our conversation was about helping to build a lasting legacy at Morgan State University. I auditioned and the difference was clear. I will always remember the first day of band camp. I received a letter, explaining that band camp registration would begin on a Sunday. Camp was to immediately follow. Nervous and excited, I remembered walking down the hall on that Saturday and seeing a lot of folks in blue, white and gold shirts. They all welcomed me to the band. Their friendly nature and conversation took my nervousness right away. Many recognized me and said, "Hey! You are the girl from the steps." I finally was realizing my dream.

My freshman year was the beginning of a growth period for the Morgan Band program. I was one of four freshman tuba players joining "M3". The first day of band camp began with an orientation. We met the director of bands and the entire staff. The orientation ended and we soon hit the field. Conditioning and commands always began on Day 1. We had outstanding senior section leadership within the band. My section leader was a female, and she was by far one of the greatest musicians I ever heard. The band members in blue and white kept us motivated. They were the first to run back to position. They marched the hardest and ensured that we were fed throughout the week. I soon found out that the students in blue and white were members of Kappa Kappa Psi National Honorary Band Fraternity and Tau Beta Sigma National Honorary Band Sorority. From the first day, I knew I desired to be a part of Tau Beta Sigma.

During my first year in the band, we had a few home games. But we traveled quite a bit, as well. My first overnight trip was to Woonsocket, Rhode Island. The excitement was clear from the time we loaded the bus. We arrived in this small town and we were treated like celebrities by the African Americans in the community. Overnight trips with the Morgan State Band always meant good, clean fun! Pillow fights and hide and seek in the hotel were a must! We were family from the beginning.

On the yard, the band was a tight-knit community. You could always identify band members because we traveled in packs and we wore our electric blue band jackets. The Morgan State campus loved our band. The highlight of my time at Morgan was the fall of 1997 when I joined Tau Beta Sigma National Honorary Band Sorority. My Epsilon Omega chapter was the top chapter in the country the year I was initiated. Through the sorority, I learned leadership, organization, friendship, sisterhood and endurance. Tau Beta Sigma made me into the woman I am today.

I was honored to serve our band program as the student assistant from 1996 to 1999. I was the band administrator and student leader. I had the honor of creating and implementing many of the organizational tools and some of the "M3" paraphernalia still used today.

After graduating, I was hired as the assistant to the director of bands. I am the first female to work as a non-auxiliary assistant band staff member. During my time, I had the opportunity handle the various business aspects of the band program, including establishing the band travel itineraries, attending various athletic meetings, adjudicating band competitions, conducting the Magnificent Marching Machine, Symphonic and Pep Band. I attribute who I am as band director, music department chair and teacher specialist to the training I received from the Director of Bands, Melvin Miles, Jr., and the Morgan State University Band program.

## About Dr. Bridgette Crawford Bell

Dr. Bridgette Crawford Bell is a Director of Band and Teacher Specialist for School Performance and Achievement in Harford County, Maryland. Bridgette is also the co-host of *The Marching Podcast*.

Bridgette, grew up in Baltimore, Maryland. She received her Bachelor of Arts (1999) and Masters of Art degrees (2005) in Music Education/Conducting from Morgan State University. While matriculating at Morgan State University, she played the tuba in the Magnificient Marching Machine "M3" Band, Pep Band, and Symphonic band. Bridgette was the tuba section leader and served as the student assistant to the director of bands from 1996 – 1999.

After graduating, Bridgette joined the Morgan State Band Staff as the Assistant to the Director of Bands from 1999 – 2012. In 1999, she also began her career as a music teacher in the Harford County School System. Bridgette has worked for the Harford County Public for the past 22 years and has taught band, orchestra and chorus. Her ensembles have received local, state and, national recognition for outstanding musicianship. Bridgette is currently a teacher specialist for school performance and achievement. In addition to her current role, Bridgette teaches graduate courses and serves a curriculum writer for the Maryland State Department of Education. She has been involved in educational and music leadership for 20+ years. Bridgette has served as department chair, adjudicator, workshop leader, clinician and private/applied instructor. She is also a trusted professional consultant for the National Teacher Board Certification for music standards.

Bridgette is a member of Tau Beta Sigma National Honorary Band Sorority (Fall 1997), Alpha Kappa Mu Honor Society (1998), Delta Sigma Theta Sorority Inc. (Spring, 2007), the National Education

Association, Maryland Music Educator Association, HBCU Band Director Consortium, and the Association of Black Woman Band Directors (Director of Membership).

# P. KEVIN WILLIAMSON

# Best Band in the Land

P. Kevin Williamson

North Carolina A&T State University

Imposter syndrome is that feeling one may get when they feel underqualified or like they don't belong. This usually occurs in the workplace, especially when one has received a promotion or joined a new organization all together. It typically attacks those who have succeeded in the first place to be in a position of responsibility and attention. A place where you feel unsure you belong. It also usually happens to women and people of color because of how society has historically tried to make us feel. I dig down deep in my heart to find the stuff I need to overcome those negative feelings when they arise. Most of that stuff I have down deep came from my faith in God and my family. It came from my mom, my dad, my sisters and brother, extended family, and close friends. The rest came from 1601 E. Market Street in Greensboro, NC, the home site of NC A&T State University and more specifically, The Blue & Gold Marching Machine. I had been on various teams and in a host of clubs, but never had I been a part of a unit so large and powerful and loving as my band. In my current job, I have had that feeling. The first thing I did was pray. The next thing I did was reflect on my time as a full, loyal member of the Blue and Gold Marching Machine.

I was first introduced to her, the band, as a little boy of 6 years old. It was during the Homecoming parade that I first saw and heard this brilliance rolling down the street. Of all the sights of the people and their attire, the sounds of laughter, radios playing, car and motorcycle engines roaring, the smells of fish frying and burgers grilling, the one thing that moved me was the marching band. As the years went on, I would hear people chanting Aggie Pride, to me it meant the band. It was all about the band. When I was considering college and was making my final decision, it came down to the band.

My band, the Blue and Gold Marching Machine. I am a product of the premier recruitment tool the university has in its possession. It got me there and keeps me around.

My experience was a whirlwind. I first joined the ranks in early August 1993. It was a hot, sunny, Sunday afternoon as I walked into Frazier Hall with no idea of what to expect. It was the first day of band camp and the room was full of young men and women from everywhere. There were mini reunions for upperclassmen as they were reunited with fellow bandmates they had not seen in several months. There was the look of welcome, care and sternness from the band staff. There was a busy, hustling energy of the student leaders made up of members of Phi Mu Alpha, Kappa Kappa Psi and Tau Beta Sigma helping to get uniform sizes, issue out instruments and other items. Then there were the blank faces of the freshmen like me. Some faces looked nervous, some seemed downright scared. There were some who were standoffish and some very welcoming, but all in all there was an overall energy that while scary was alluring.

My first year was spent getting to know my section and other members of the band and how to navigate this new side of my life with academics. I was blown away by the fact that only a small percentage of the band, around 15 percent, were actually music majors making it a truly cross curricular environment. This realization motivated me to take my classes more seriously and take an overall more proactive approach to learning. I firmly believe this mix in academic pursuits combined with the blended regional cultures and economic backgrounds created an even richer experience for me and others sharing this experience with me. I was exposed to students from all over the country with a variety of perspectives and day to day expectations. I was afforded the opportunity to travel to places I may have never seen had I not been a member of this amazing organization. I had siblings and friends, but never would I have imagined feeling like I had hundreds of sisters and brothers. I recall an upperclassman pulling me to the side because he thought I looked out of sorts. He simply said, "Kev, whatever is going on with you, know and remember you have about 200 brothers and sisters who have your back!" The feeling of belonging and community I felt in that moment had never been stronger in my life. I was all in and drinking the Kool-Aid®.

To quote the legendary "Iron" Mike Tyson, "Discipline is doing what you hate to do, but do it like you love it!" As a member of the Blue and Gold Marching Machine discipline was everything. For non-believers in discipline, the struggle was real with regard to performance. No matter how talented or gifted you are, with no discipline, something is going to suffer. I learned this lesson early, the hard way. If you don't do cardio, you will not have the appropriate wind to play your instrument while marching or dancing. If you don't practice your music outside of rehearsals you will be called out and not allowed on the field for the halftime show. I saw this happen, not to me, but to a friend. If you don't treat your body right outside of practice, it will tell on you during performance times. This has carried over into my grown-up professional life.

Ill preparation has consequences. Those consequences can range from a little to a lot of embarrassment to life changing ones. The discipline learned was such a major part of my growth. Grit was built into our daily routines and was necessary to get through most field rehearsals. "It always seems impossible until it's done." – Nelson Mandela. Grit is that extra something that we find deep inside and build up through hard work and determination. Grit is about sustained, consistent effort toward a goal even when we struggle, falter, or temporarily fail. Resilience is our ability to bounce back after we have struggled, faltered, or failed. I have been able to build and strengthen these muscles and my participation in the band was a large part of that training. Teamwork was paramount. We learned that as a band we move as one unit on the same page. We learned at a high level that each member must do their part if we are to be successful. Loyalty was our motto and way of life. We were loyal to the band and her efforts. This loyalty meant staying committed throughout band camp and the entire season. In fact, during that era of the band, in order to receive a gold Loyalty T-shirt, one would need to have completed the full two weeks of band camp.

It was one of the first symbols of pride from being a part of this unit that you wore on your chest. It was a heavy wear because it was earned and it helped make dedication clear and more than an expectation from our leadership, but a desire from within. Regarding leadership, some of the best examples came from my band director, the late great Dr. Johnny B. Hodge, Jr., Doc, as we referred to him, showed us the good and bad of being in charge. As I lead committees and teams in my professional life, I recall many examples I observed in Doc. Doc was very direct, yet fair in his decisions. Decision making and direct communication is imperative to directing a team to achieve desired results. Doc would usually be in the band room before we were and was usually there after we were gone. I learned that solid leaders arrive early and stay late. I learned the hard way that punctuality was not suggested but required. To be early is to be on time, to be on time is to be late and to be late is to be ready for the next rehearsal (and to run laps). The running lap's part was mine.

The life lessons learned from my time in the band cannot be replaced. I cannot imagine my life without the experiences, good and not so good. The skills, the wisdom, the laughs and the lifelong friendships have all impacted my life in immeasurable ways. Outside of church and pledging Phi Mu Alpha and Omega Psi Phi, there is no one organization that I reflect upon with so much joy, love and pride. Yes, Aggie Pride!

I will drop this one here for my BGMM family. "Glad to see you again, I haven't seen you since I don't know when, we are the Marching Aggie Band and we are the Best band, best band, best band in the land!"

## About P. Kevin Williamson

In his current role at UNC Greensboro, P. Kevin oversees the Development team in the Division of University Advancement. He and his team work to support campus wide initiatives to include all the academic units as well as nonacademic areas such the University Libraries and the Weatherspoon Art Museum. He has a background in the management of major gifts, annual giving, leadership annual giving, planned giving, corporate and foundation relations, parent & family giving and prospect management & research.

A native of High Point, NC, P. Kevin is a graduate of NC A&T State University with a degree in English. Following graduation from NC A&T, he worked as a District Executive for the Boy Scouts of America for several years until transitioning into Higher Education philanthropy in 2007 where he served as Director of Development for Leadership Gifts at UNC Wilmington. He has since moved around the UNC System having served in other roles at UNC Greensboro, WSSU and back to UNC Wilmington into the role of Assistant Vice Chancellor for Major Gifts, returned to his alma mater as Assistant Vice Chancellor for Strategic Development and in May of 2022 returned to UNC Greensboro as Associate Vice Chancellor for Development. P. Kevin resides in High Point, NC with his wife of 19 years, Tia, their daughters Trinity and Winter, and two miniature schnauzers, Sacha and Audo.

# JASON GILLIARD

# Living a Dyn-O-mite Life
## Ongoing Journey of Self-discovery

**Jason Gilliard**

**Alcorn State University**

My love for marching band began at a very young age. I was born in Atlanta, GA, and grew up with a deep passion for music. My grandparents often made me play the piano and drums at our family church. My mother noticed that the only activity I never gave up on was band. While I loved sports, I didn't have the same passion to compete in them. However, when I discovered marching band, in 1995 after seeing the Morris Brown Marching Wolverines, I knew exactly what I wanted to do!

I started my band journey in 6th grade at Forest Park Middle School. Our band teacher had us all pick three instruments we wanted to play and gave us a mouthpiece to "test our potential." I knew I wanted to play the saxophone, and that was it. I chose the saxophone, tuba, and flute. However, she thought I was best suited for the tuba, so that's what I ended up with. I mastered it and became the best in the class. Nevertheless, I still had a strong desire to be a saxophonist, mostly due to my love for Jazz. Fortunately, my family relocated to DeKalb County, and in the 7th grade, I enrolled at Shamrock Middle School (formerly Shamrock High School and now Druid Hill Middle School). I asked the band teacher there if I could switch to the saxophone, and he graciously allowed me to do so. I am forever grateful for that opportunity. He was also my first introduction to a male music educator! Under his guidance, I was able to learn and expand my talent. By the end of 7th grade, I had self-taught myself to play all the other woodwind instruments. He also allowed us to play with the high school band during their homecoming performance, under the direction of Mr. Kevin Jones. I was overjoyed and knew I was going to Druid Hills High School to be a part of the Marching Red Devils! Mr. Jones was the first black male music teacher I had, and I am forever grateful for all that he allowed us to experience. He is a graduate of Clark-Atlanta University and introduced us to CAU, Morris Brown, Southern University, FAMU, Bethune-Cookman, Jackson State, and many other HBCUs and their marching programs.

I had plans to attend Morris Brown College for years, and I must admit that being involved in a small part of the filming of Drumline solidified my decision to march in college. However, I found my true home at Alcorn State University. I remember showing up to the audition completely unprepared because in my mind, I knew I was the best. I played several instruments, was 1st chair, played in All-state, and could sight-read exceptionally well! Mr. Samuel S. Griffin (Rest in Musical Peace) quickly humbled me that day. He was intimidating. The way Griff would look at you before he opened his mouth could make you crumble, but even when he critiqued you, he did it with purpose. Griff recognized potential in individuals, but he pushed us to reach beyond that potential. When I reflect on my years at Alcorn State, I feel an overwhelming amount of pride, joy, and gratitude.

Mr. Samuel Griffin taught me how to face my life decisions, deal with them, grow through them, and strive to be better each day. As a freshman, I had a quiet "Devin Miles" attitude. I wasn't boldly obnoxious and didn't say much, but my attitude was present. I enrolled at Alcorn State in the Fall of 2003, alongside a large incoming Atlanta class. It was reassuring to see so many familiar faces from DeKalb County in Mississippi. However, I showed up late on my second day of freshman year band camp, and I can still feel the pain from those jumping jacks to this day! Mr. Jones used to tell us all the time, "Early is on time, on time is late, and late is unacceptable." I'm not sure why I didn't carry that with me into the first week of college, but on that second day, I learned quickly that it wasn't just something my high school director said—it was something Griff lived by.

One of the greatest experiences of attending an HBCU was being surrounded by people who looked like me, talked like me, and understood my journey without judgment for my mistakes along the way. They embraced me, made mistakes with me, taught me how to be comfortable with myself, and allowed me the space and time to discover my path in life. I won't lie and say freshman year was easy—it was tough! I had a hard time adjusting during the first part of the fall semester. I was juggling band practice and classes, and initially, I was scared to interact with anyone. However, my section leader at the time pulled me aside around the 3rd or 4th game and had a conversation with me about opening up and letting things be. I was closed off and stuck in my shell. After that conversation, I decided to clean myself up and just be me, and that's when I found my lifelong friends.

Being a part of the Sounds of Dyn-O-mite gave me the opportunity to travel to places I never thought I'd be able to go. My love for travel and music intertwined beautifully! We went to St. Louis, Washington, DC, Delaware, Virginia, and more. During those years, I realized that I was probably in the best shape of my life. I used to think PT (physical training) was just running a few laps, doing some sit-ups, and jumping jacks, and calling it a day. Griff worked us out and made sure we could withstand the Mississippi heat and the arctic cold. At the time, I didn't fully understand it, but as you start to live your life, you find yourself referencing your HBCU experiences in everything you do. The things I learned from Alcorn State were resilience, perseverance, nobility, adaptability, and, most importantly, being pushed out of my comfort zone to take on the world. I am forever grateful for my experience, and I wouldn't want to change anything about it because I'm not sure if I would have shaped into the person I am today without it.

I want to express my gratitude to every single person I ever encountered, even those not-so-positive experiences. They were all necessary. However, without the love and support from my fellow HBCU graduates and Alcorn alumni, I might be living a very different life. The life I live now is incredibly rewarding, and it's all because of my experiences in an HBCU band, surrounded by HBCU culture and excellence!

Thank you to all of you who shaped me during my time at Alcorn and beyond.

# About Jason Gilliard

Jason is a native of Atlanta, GA and is a product of Dekalb County Schools. They are a graduate of Druid Hills High School and began their studies at Alcorn State University in 2003 majoring in Mathematics Education. During their time at Alcorn State University, they were part of the Sounds of Dyn-O-mite Marching Band in the Saxophone section and participated in the Pep band, Symphonic band, True Illusions dance team, and Math & Science Club.

Jason Currently Lives in Dallas, TX where he is the Texas Area Supervisor for Alto Pharmacy. They have helped to launch several pharmacy sites, including Long Island, Dallas, Houston, Austin, New York, and San Diego. They are determined to help fulfil the company's mission which is "to fulfill Medicine's true purpose – to improve quality of life – for everyone who needs it."

They are involved their local community with several organizations to help improve equality for everyone such as Dallas Area Habitat for Humanity, HRC Texas, Promise House, Community Advisor Board, and Alto Cares.

# HAMILTON GRANT

# Lessons From Behind the Whistle
## Hamilton Grant
### South Carolina State University

Growing up in South Carolina, I have always been mesmerized by the sounds and rhythms of the Marching 101 Band from South Carolina State University. Their unique combination of dancing and marching mixed with the iconic compositions of Mr. Ronald J. Sargent would have me in awe any time that I was privileged to see them. While I loved the boom of the Bongo Brothers, the confidence of Amtrak Express and of course the grace and class of the Champagne Dancers, my focus would always seem to zoom in on the drum majors. While not large in numbers, the Caped Crusaders had a larger-than-life persona. The ability to command respect from their peers, perform with unmatched enthusiasm and lead the 101 into battle captivated me.

My father who at the time served the University as a Trustee Member recognized this curiosity that I had with the 101 and decided to surprise me during a home football game. Unbeknownst to me, my father was going to introduce me to the Director of Bands after halftime. What neither of us knew was that Mr. Sargent would not only let me sit and engage with the drum majors, but he asked if I would help conduct the 101's staple song, "Up For The Bulldogs!" While I say this with humor, much like how high school seniors in sports have a commitment day, this one experience solidified my commitment to attend the University while a student in elementary school.

As I got older and began my musical journey as an instrumentalist in middle and high school, when it came down to looking at colleges to attend, my decision was clear. In the fall of 2007, I became a proud freshman in the SC State Marching 101 Band! Joining this family of

320 members was undoubtedly one of the biggest highlights of my collegiate tenure, but there was still some unfinished business. As a 5'11" rising Junior, nervous but determined, I committed myself to trying out for drum major. After an intense process of cardio, precision marching and leadership evaluations, I achieved a lifelong dream of becoming a Caped Crusader! For two years, I was blessed to lead some of the best musicians and leaders from our institution as a member of this squad. While I lived in the moment of marching out a childhood fantasy instilled in me by Mr. Sargent, what I didn't know was that this student led role was preparing me for my life to come. Here are just a few takeaways that have served as a foundation in leadership for me from this experience.

Your communication skills should always be under construction. Have you ever traveled down a road that always seems to have some sort of work being done to it? While inconvenient in nature, it's necessary to safely carry you to your destination. Communication works the same way. It is not enough to simply give a verbal command, but can you convey a message that strikes fire and determination to your audience. I can remember as a rookie drum major my first time addressing the band from the podium. Nervous but determined to get my point across, I mounted the podium to give the announcements to end rehearsal. It was an epic failure. While the band respected the podium, it was obvious from my vantage point that my message was not getting across. It was then that my head drum major pulled me to the side and gave me this nugget of wisdom. "Authority does equate to yelling." My message didn't land because I thought that because I was in a position of power, my approach was to be stern when if I would have just been myself and gave my message with confidence, it would have been received a lot better. This began a humbling journey of always working to perfect my communication skills. Little did I know that this lesson would help me to persuade thousands of people to vote for me in a local election almost 10 years later.

Serving in capacity as drum major also taught me very early into my experience that there was a clear distinction between obligatory leadership and effective leadership. Before serving as a drum major, I could remember watching drum majors in years past and noticing how certain ones had more of a connection with the band than others. There were individuals who went the extra mile to ensure that everyone felt seen and performed at the highest level. While the band felt more of a connection to certain individuals, the band never disrespected those who they didn't feel that connection with. This was a real-life example to the layers of leadership. In life, people respect the seat of authority but depending on the approach, whoever holds that seat can lose the respect of those they are in authority of. We are obligated to follow certain titles that have a level of power, but it takes a special leader to persuade followers to want to follow them.

If you've ever marched in an HBCU band, you know how music rehearsals can go. It's for that reason that you grow to appreciate those who grace the podium that can keep you engaged for what can seem like hours of repetitive learning. I can remember one of our assistant directors using the analogy while conducting a crescendo that "you can't serve wine before its time." While said to paint a picture that kept you intrigued in dynamics, thinking back I can't help but to draw the correlation in this analogy and young leaders. If you know anything about wine, it takes several steps to get to the finished product that you purchase. This is because each phase in the creation of wine must be treated with caution and patience. If a step is missed or rushed, it will destroy the wine and significantly disqualify the product. In my experience, rushing and skipping steps for young leaders can and will disqualify you from future opportunities, much like wine. A mentor once told me that "young leaders are like film; they just need a little bit of exposure to develop. But if that exposure happens too fast, the picture is ruined." So often as a millennial eager to show the world my potential and poise, I have tried to expedite my process in leadership not knowing that skipping steps in my process would consequently delay it. Growing comfortable with your individual process of growth is an unnerving feeling because it comes with the uncertainty of not knowing your timeline. We set goals for ourselves with deadlines to accomplish but often don't consider necessary detours that teach us worthwhile lessons. The best leader is an experienced leader, and every experience isn't a great one. Shifting your perspective to appreciate your own growth process rather than your desired timeline will remove the blinders of leadership in your individual lives. Young leaders who are exposed to too much too quickly could potentially ruin their own trajectory and those in their same age range. This requires a level of maturity that could serve as a trampoline for your personal and professional growth. "You can't serve wine before it's time."

Many outside of our world of band will only look at its members as those who perform on Saturday and Sunday events. What they don't see is the level of training that goes into each and everything that is done. As I grow older, I find myself daily using these lessons learned while in college in my everyday routine of life. I'm beyond grateful for my HBCU band experience and quite honestly don't know where I would be in life without it. Each member of our band and staff has left an indelible mark on my life and has shaped me to be the leader I am today.

## About Hamilton Grant

Hamilton Grant is a businessman, community leader and strategist with over 15 years of experience in business administration and finance. Hamilton's ability to provide innovative solutions to complex problems has made him a highly sought after leader in the areas of business strategy and servant leadership. Mr. Grant's wealth of relationships and experience can be a valued asset to your company's development and growth. Hamilton holds a Bachelor of Arts Degree in Business Marketing from South Carolina State University and a Masters of Business Administration Degree from Alabama A&M University.

Hamilton's experiences and accomplishments include but are not limited to:

- Columbia Monthly Magazine's Best and Brightest Under 35

- SC Black Pages 20 Under 40

- SC State University 40 Under 40 Inaugural Class

- Columbia Metropolitan Magazine's Top 10 Young Professionals

- Columbia Chamber of Commerce Leadership Columbia Advisory Board

- Columbia Museum of Art Board of Trustees

- Former SC State University Board of Trustees

- Former President of the Columbia Urban League Young Professionals

Hamilton is also a proud member of Omega Psi Phi Fraternity, Incorporated and Kappa Kappa Psi National Honorary Band Fraternity.

# CALEB T. DUNBAR

# Joys of the Jukebox
## Caleb T. Dunbar
### Southern University A&M College

"SSSSSS U! Whooo! S S S S S S U! Rep who? Rep Southern U?" Let's just say our chant was a little more aggressive while I was at Southern University (If you know you know). A little over 14 years ago I began my journey at THE Southern University Agricultural and Mechanical College at Baton Rouge. I can recall graduating from high school in May 2008 and instantly getting excited about going to Southern University. I could not wait for orientation. I was only 17 at the time and would not turn 18 until a few days after moving in. I could not wait to have that freedom of being on my own, meeting new people, having new experiences, trying new foods, football games, tailgates, the after parties, and finally getting a taste of "A Different World." At the time I didn't know a whole lot about the school but I knew it had a great band, a great business school, and plenty of people who look like me. Having a school where the majority of the people were like me was very important. After graduating from a high school where the student body was very mixed, I was very eager to be a part of an environment that was created for me. Southern University has been in my family for generations. After all, my grandfather, mother, uncle, and older cousins all attended The Southern University Agricultural and Mechanical College and it was now my turn. The only difference is, I would be the first one in my family to attend and be a part of the Southern University Marching Band.

Throughout my years on the yard, I was heavily involved in band, the college of business, and being a jaguar ambassador. Out of all of these experiences, I must say that being a member of the Southern

University March Band "The Human Jukebox" gave me some of the most memorable experiences and lifelong friendships.

## My Story

July 2008 came around and I was working at my local grocery store and my high school band director came in and asked where I was attending college. I told him that I was attending Southern University in Baton Rouge and his eyes opened wide and he said "Great, you should really consider auditioning for the band." Keep in mind this is one month before the freshmen move in date, I was only thinking about orientation and moving into my dorm. I had no clue how to set up a band audition with a college or if that was even something I could do late in the summer. I called the campus and asked to speak with the band director. After a few phone calls I was able to contact the band director. This is when I first came in contact with Dr. Lawrence Jackson who was the Director of Bands at the time.

Very shakenly, I remember mumbling my name and where I was from. I further went on to ask Dr. Jackson if it was too late to audition for the band. He went into detail that it was really late in the audition season but asked if I could be ready to audition during student orientation. I excitedly said yes. Orientation day came and that excitement turned into nervousness. The first time I walked in the band room I remember thinking "It's really cold in here, this band hall is huge, and the person auditioning ahead of me is playing something very technical." I instantly thought, "Yea, I'll just leave back out and they won't even know who I was." Before I could leave Mr. Nathan Haymer came in and said "Are you ready?" I said "I may as well be." The audition went on and they said I should expect a band camp letter in a week or so. Little did I know, this one audition would be leading me to four years of band memories that would further enhance my HBCU experience.

A few weeks before band camp I would begin to work out more, practice my instrument more, and watch a few videos I could find on the internet in hopes that I could be as prepared as possible. No matter what I did to prepare, I quickly learned that nothing can prepare you for the experiences that you will have or lessons you will learn while being a member of an HBCU Marching Band, especially the Human Jukebox.

Going into the band as a crab (a freshmen band member), there were a lot of adjustments for me. The Southern University Marching Band is a very well known, flashy and show style marching band. The expectation is high knees, kicking on eight, high quality sound, high energy and more. I was coming in from a core style marching band who only knew core style which included roll step and duck walk. I think it's safe to say this was an adjustment. I was excited to learn a new style, for this is the style of band that I always wanted in high school. Not only did I learn a new marching style, I learned how to be more accountable and how to hold my own. "Every tub has to sit on its own bottom" is something that was commonly echoed through the band hall and this is something that sticks with me to this day. As the years went on there were many lessons taught, experiences gained, and of this can be attributed to me staying in college to continue the pursuit of my degree.

**Joys of the Jukebox**

During my time in the band, I was able to perform for a couple Saints NFL games, march in the Disney World Parade, march in the biggest Mardi Gras parades, rock the stands every football game, battle the opposing bands week after week, and also be a part of the brass choir in the spring. Here is where I learned the meaning of commitment, "finishing the course" and holding my own. Thanks to the Southern University Marching Band, "The Human Jukebox '' I was exposed to different genres of music and I also learned the importance of building new bonds with people I didn't know. I began to quickly process a lot of commands in a short amount of time. I now have lifelong friends, a certain pride about my university and myself, quotes that get me through tough situations, and another reason to always be an advocate for Historically Black Colleges and Universities. Many lessons that were learned in the Isaac Greggs Band Hall have been applied to my post graduate and life experiences. I was taught hard work, accountability, and to stand on my own. This has carried over to my current workplace that allows me to excel at work and I am able to handle all things that come my way.

I am very thankful for the Southern University Marching Band and Southern University. I wear my blue and gold with pride. I am currently a Lifetime Member of the Human Jukebox Alumni Association. I still enjoy Jaguar football, watching the current edition of the band marching up and down the field, and seeing our university continue to grow in excellence. We have Alumni support unlike any other. I love all Historically Black Colleges and Universities but there is nothing like Southern University. We are truly the "Defenders of the Gold and Blue" and we mean it when we say "Nobody Does It Better" Southern University is home and the Southern University Marching Band is "Often Imitated but Never Duplicated.

So, I encourage all who read this book to learn more about The Southern University System and the Southern University Marching Band and come visit us on the bluff where you can learn more about our traditions, legacy, and purpose and how to connect with the university in the future. Here on the bluff, WE ARE ONE!

# About Caleb T. Dunbar

Caleb Dunbar was born and raised in Jonesville, La and is a current resident of Baton Rouge, La. He is a Fall 2012 graduate of Southern University A&M College where he was a part of the fall 2008 crab class of The Southern University March Band also known as "The Human Jukebox" where he played Trumpet. He was also active in the Black Executive Exchange program also known as (B.E.E.P.). He was also a student ambassador/orientation leader.

He has obtained a Bachelor of Science in Marketing from the College of Business. Since graduation, he has obtained a Master's of Business Administration with a Specialization in Human Resource Management from Ashford University and a Bachelor in Theology from H.O.P.E. Bible Institute, Baton Rouge, La. Caleb is currently employed by the Louisiana Department of Education as a Budget Manager.

He is also the owner of Caleb T. Dunbar Photography, LLC. Caleb is a member of the Breath of Life Church pastored by June Mays Gayden where he serves as a board member and on the media team. He is very excited to share his experience at The Southern University A&M College.

# FAYESHA COLE

# My Passion and Purpose

Fayesha Cole

Norfolk State University

I would have never thought that choosing to play the flute when I was in the 6th grade would lead to me finding my passion and purpose. I started off at Falling Creek Elementary School in Chesterfield, Virginia. I continued my musical education when I went to Meadowbrook High School in Chesterfield, Virginia. I became the first African American Drum Major of the marching band. Then is when I knew that this was something I wanted to do for life.

Norfolk State University was my only choice of colleges. I remember people saying, "why are you going to that party school?" My dad told me not to pay them any attention, so I didn't. A little-known secret is that I had never seen the Norfolk State Spartan Legion before I joined the band. I knew I wanted to major in Music Ed. so, with that being said, I had to send in an audition tape. My Minister of Music and I spent hours in the church recording and re-recording my audition tape. It was time well spent because my tuition books and fees were paid in full with a band scholarship.

I remember the day my parents and brother dropped me off at the Twin Towers. This is where I met my roommate and now lifelong friend, Danielle Yonkers. Ironically, she was majoring in music and was going to be in the band as well. I remember our parents exchanging phone numbers and the rest was history.

This was the beginning of something special for me. Music had always been the one thing that I was good at doing and where I always felt accepted. Well, the next day was the first day of band camp. Danielle and I woke up bright and early to be at the band room at 6:00 am. This was an amazing feeling. I was thinking to myself, I get to do the one thing I love to do all day long. I was excited about life.

I marched the first game ever in Dick Price stadium in the summer of 1997. The feeling that came over me was something I had never felt before and I knew I wanted to keep feeling it. I was addicted to the adrenaline rush. I was addicted to the cheers of the crowd. I was addicted to the way I was able to make people feel through my instrument.

The band staff at NSU were amazing. They were our parents while we were away from home. My matriculation through NSU and my success is largely credited to them. These are the people that helped me find my passion. They're the people that showed me how important a person in their role means in the life of a student. Each director and assistant brought something unique to the table.

Mr. Oneil Sanford who we affectionately called "Doc" was the Director of Bands. He led with passion and he taught with the love of a father. He disciplined as he should and we knew when to straighten up. Doc took the time to learn from each of his students and could call us all by name. We would have many talks that had nothing to do about music but about practical life. He could have a conversation with each of our parents and have personal knowledge about where we were academically and musically at the time. He could also tell them what he thought we needed to be successful. One of my most vivid moments with him was when I finished my master's degree and told him I would be moving to Richmond because I got a job with Richmond Public Schools. He looked at me as if he were truly hurt. He said, "I thought you would stick around here a little bit longer." I remember feeling like I had hurt him because I was moving on. Even though I was no longer in his office every day he still kept track of how I was doing. It was when I received my first high school teaching job, I realized how hard it is to teach inner city kids. It truly bothered me, as my parents always provided for me, and I lacked nothing. To see the other side was a harsh reality for me. I sent out a mass email to everyone in my address book requesting help to get my students to the High Stepping National Band Competition. Doc called me in the middle of the workday to tell me that I had to learn not to take every situation with the students on as my own. It took me a while to understand what he was saying to me, but I eventually understood. To this day, I get calls from Dr. Sanford checking on me and my children. He always tells me how proud he is of me. Every time I hear his voice, I have that same admiration as I did when I was 18 and he spoke to me.

The Assistant Director of Bands, Mr. Paul I. Adams was a peculiar man. He had no other choice than to be that way due to the music he has going around in his head. Mr. Adams is a master composer and arranger. His work is known across the world. I was a student conductor for the wind ensemble. I loved having that responsibility. I was always complimented on my conducting styles and inflections. Mr. Adams didn't care about any of that. He would ask hard questions to you while you were on the podium in front of your peers that would make your heart pound out of your chest. As a result of his tough love, when I became a band director, I was able to stand on the podium in any situation with confidence. When Mr. Adams calls, I answer and I listen.

Another Assistant Director was Ms. Stephanie Sanders. She was known to be a loud southern girl that could pick up any woodwind instrument and play like she was born with it. Even though I had a woman as a high school band director, I never had a black woman, with feminine qualities and the type of leadership that Ms. Sanders possessed. She would stand in front of the Marching Band with confidence and lead with a passion that no one could cut off. I was always amazed by her talent and leadership. When I got the interview for the Director of Bands Job at Virginia Union University, I called Ms. Sanders and asked her how I should dress, how I should do my makeup along with a host of other questions. When my dad died, Ms. Sanders drove to Richmond for the funeral.  I will always have a special admiration for Ms. Stephanie Sanders.

I gave the above examples to show how being a part of the NSU Spartan Legion helped me find my passion and my purpose.  While my official job title is Director of Bands, I do so much more.  Not because it's part of the contract, but because I see it necessary for the growth of my students.  My purpose in life is to bridge adolescence to adulthood through music education.  I love this job because it never gets boring and it's always evolving.  When I wake up to go to work, I don't dread it one bit.  I'm excited to see what the day will bring and what new challenges we will have to work out.

Thank you to Norfolk State University for accepting me and filling my educational toolbox.  Thank you to the Spartan Legion Band Staff for giving me the strength to be successful in this crazy thing called life.  Lastly, thank you God for allowing me to work "in" my purpose every day.

## About Fayesha Cole


"Motherly" is one word that is consistently used when describing her teaching style. "Driven" is used when describing her work ethic."

Fayesha Cole, Director of Bands at Virginia Union University, is a Richmond native with family ties to Virginia Union University; her parents, who are alumni, met there. Music has always kept her motivated. Fayesha started her music career at Falling Creek Middle School when she decided to play the flute. From the 6th grade she has been an active music student. She even became the first African American Drum of Meadowbrook High School in Chesterfield, Virginia. She earned a bachelor's and master's Degree from Norfolk State University in Music Education.   As a proud member of Tau Beta Sigma National Honorary Band Sorority Incorporated, bridging students from adolescence to adulthood through music education is her life's goal. She has earned superior ratings in District Assessment as a middle and high school teacher.

Fayesha made a major change in jobs when she was chosen to work at Virginia Union University. She was chosen to be Director of Bands and tasked to build a marching band from the ground up. Under her leadership, the band is known all through the United States for its clean sound and innovative approach to field show design. The ensemble is known as AOS, the Ambassadors of Sound Marching Band and is flourishing and growing with each season.

# QUINTON M. JOYNER

# AHHHH, Kick Back! Viking Attack! ! !

Quinton M. Joyner

Elizabeth City State University

Pause!  Before we get into my HBCU Band Experience, I think I should tell you how I ended up there.  Truthfully, I didn't know about HBCUs as a high school student.  See, my parents didn't go to college and neither did any of my older siblings.  I made good grades but didn't fully understand the process of getting admitted to a four-year university.  Anyway, one day, my teacher, Mrs. Woodham, asked me, "Quinton!  What do you plan to do after graduation?"  I, being my sarcastic self, told her, "I think I'm going to get a job at Hackney (a nearby factory) and work the rest of my life."  I had no idea that she took that response seriously.  Later in the semester, I was sitting in class, when the intercom asked for Quinton Joyner to report to Guidance.  I left class and went to meet with Mr. Hodge, the Guidance Counselor.  He told me to report to the cafeteria to speak with someone here to see me.  Confused, I did as I was told.  When I entered the cafeteria, there was a man who introduced himself as Tony Price.  Mr. Price asked me to talk with him for a minute.  He asked me various questions about my educational experience at Chocowinity High School.  Most of the conversation revolved around the band.  Once we finished our conversation, he informed me that based on the information I gave him, he had filled out my application to Elizabeth City State University.  He told me the application fee would be waived and I should receive an official acceptance letter with information about my financial aid shortly.  He was correct.  I was accepted and received ample financial aid in the forms of grants and scholarships to attend Elizabeth City State University.

Elizabeth City State University was a simple yet beautiful campus placed firmly in the northeastern part of North Carolina.  It was close enough that you could experience busier cities but not close enough that you would be distracted.  Arriving on campus, I checked into my dormitory and proceeded to move into my room.  However, I was on the 3rd floor of Womack Hall and the building was too old to have an elevator.  I was glad that we didn't have our freshman band orientation until later that evening.  We were meeting in Moore Hall Auditorium because there was a fire over the summer, in Williams Hall (the Music Department) and it wasn't cleared for re-entry.  I arrived at the auditorium alone, entered and took my seat in the middle right section.  Some upperclassmen came over and introduced themselves before we began.  The meeting started and I realized that I was definitely starting all over.  I looked around the auditorium and didn't know one, single person.  As we all introduced ourselves, people who were upperclassmen in the "Sound of Class" would make noise and cheer for the freshman who came from the same high school band programs as themselves.  Of course, when I introduced myself, I didn't get any applause or cheer, because who has ever heard of Chocowinity.  The upperclassmen went over the expectations and itinerary for the next day, the first real day of band camp.

On a hot Monday morning in August 1996, they began band camp with 6:00am calisthenics.  I say they because I wasn't there.  I had to go to my job at Hardee's on the Outer Banks, which I had no idea was that far from campus.  After that drive, I realized that was not going to happen.  I returned to campus to find the band in music rehearsal in the gym.  I was late.  So, I didn't have any music or idea what was going on.  My section leader gave me the music and a place in the section.  I played 2nd part and sat last chair.  I was fine with this for the time being because I didn't know how hard the music was.

Band camp progressed with daily calisthenics, music rehearsals and marching practice.  The high knee lift and dancing made marching practice harder than I had ever experienced.  Though it was difficult, I was getting better at it.  However, I hated being at Elizabeth City State University.  It wasn't the actual university that I disliked.  I was becoming homesick and missing my friends.  I called home every night to talk to my mom. I would ask her if I could come home and attend East Carolina University, which was about thirty minutes from home. She told me to give it one more week and if I still didn't like it, I could come home. It was a deal and I was counting down the days!

One day, a new student arrived at camp. She was from the local high school, Northeastern, played alto sax and already had friends in the band. She played 2nd part and sat beside me. We introduced ourselves and I learned her name was Kassi. We quickly became friends. Besides our love of marching band, we were both music majors and had similar taste in food, music and entertainment. After making friends with Kassi, I didn't feel as homesick and wasn't missing my friends as much. She was the first friend I made at ECSU but she was far from the last. Needless to say, I didn't go home when my mom told me I could.

As the season progressed, I moved from the alto sax to mellophone. I really don't know what I was thinking because that meant I had to relearn all the music and memorize it. This all happened right before homecoming. We were finishing up the dance routine for homecoming and the upperclassmen said that we needed to learn "The Viking Attack!" I had no idea what it was but I was intrigued. The upperclassmen began to teach, what is to this day, my favorite band dance. It began with yelling at the top of our lungs, "AHHHH, Kick Back! Viking Attack!" It was easy to learn, because the words were the commands! It was one of those all-purpose dances; good for a halftime, parade or spirit mix. The past editions of the "Sound of Class" had performed it and it was a small connection to our predecessors.

The marching band season ended with the announcement, we were losing our director. The department chair, Dr. Floyd L. Robinson, told us that they were going to search for a new director and we would meet the candidates that were contenders. Until the hire of the new director, he would serve as our symphonic wind ensemble director. I worked in the Music Department office for Dr. Robinson. He was more than a band director, he was a music educator to his very core. He taught me about the responsibilities of being a director. He sent me to my first IMA (Intercollegiate Music Association) and made sure that I attended all four years of undergraduate career. Under his direction, the ECSU Symphonic Wind Ensemble went on an annual spring tour, where we traveled the eastern seaboard performing and recruiting at various high schools. By the end of freshman year, Elizabeth City State University was feeling like home to me.

Over the next three years, I grew to love ECSU even more. After summer break, the SOC was under the direction of Mr. Ivory Brock. He moved the band into an entirely new direction. The "Sound of Class" took our name very seriously. It was present in our appearance, and behavior as a band program. He gave me an opportunity to serve the band as a section leader. He made us constantly prove that we deserved to be in a leadership position. He also taught me a ridiculous amount about being a band director. Much of what I learned, I still use today in the classroom. Mr. Brock teamed up with a new assistant director, Mr. Au. He arranged and taught several of our arrangements. I made several friends in and outside the band. Spring 1998, I became a member of the Gamma Rho Chapter of Phi Beta Sigma Fraternity, Inc. I gained an entirely new family of brothers and sisters. During my time as an undergrad, I served as Step Master, Dean of Pledges and Chapter President. Each year, I looked forward to events like homecoming, the Greek probates and Viking Fest. I maintained a good working relationship with my professors, who would continuously stay on me about my academics and my GPA. The Music Department professors worked diligently to make sure that we were prepared for the world we were about to face as graduates of the university. Dr. Robinson, Mr. Brock, Dr. Brown, Dr. Knight, Mr. Au and Mr. Corozine all worked diligently to increase our knowledge and motivate us. My time at

Elizabeth City State University redirected my entire future and I will cherish that experience for the rest of my life.

## About Quinton M. Joyner

Quinton Joyner is a native of Chocowinity, NC but currently resides in Graham, NC. He is a product of Beaufort County Schools, specifically Chocowinity High School. After graduation, Quinton attended Elizabeth City State University to obtain a Bachelor's Degree in Music with a Minor in Education, Concentration Instrumental in the fall of 1996. He participated in the ECSU Marching "Sound of Class", Symphonic Wind Ensemble and the ECSU Pep Band. As a freshman, Quinton played Alto Saxophone for half of the marching season then switched to French horn to finish out the year. In the marching and pep band, Quinton served as French horn section leader for his Junior and Senior years. His senior year, he won Outstanding French Horn and Outstanding Brasswind for the 1999 Marching Season. While at Elizabeth City State University, he served as the President of the Collegiate Music Educators National Conference (CMENC). Spring 1998, Quinton was initiated in the Gamma Rho Chapter of Phi Beta Sigma Fraternity, Inc. As a member of the chapter, he held the positions of Dean of Pledges, Step Master and Chapter President. Quinton finished the Bachelor of Arts in Music with a Minor in Education program and received his degree as a part of the class of 2000.

After graduating from ECSU, Quinton began his teaching career as a Band Director in Martin County Schools at Roanoke Middle School and Roanoke High School. Two years later in 2002, he decided to pursue a Master's Degree in Music Education from Thee Jackson State University in Jackson, Mississippi. During his time at Jackson, Quinton was under the tutelage of Dr. Lewis Liddell, Dr. Ralph Chapman, Dr. Michael Magruder, Mr. Dowell Taylor, and several others. His time at Jackson State helped refine his perspective on the various musical ensembles. Quinton finished the

Master of Music Education Program in one year and received his degree as a part of the class of 2003.

Upon his return to North Carolina in August 2003, Quinton accepted a job as Director of Bands at Warren County Middle School. Under his direction, the middle school band won Excellent and Superior ratings.  He also served as the assistant director to Taylor Whitehead, the director of Warren County High School "Dynamic Marching Machine".  In 2009, Quinton left Warren County to teach in Burlington, North Carolina at Broadview Middle School and Cummings High School.  During his nine years there, the high school band competed throughout the state and won several awards. Quinton taught for one year in Guilford County before arriving at his current position.

In 2019, Quinton became the Director of Bands at Lucas Middle School in Durham, NC.  He was named Lucas Middle School Teacher of the Year for the 2021-2022 School Year.  He currently serves as Director of Bands, Team Chair and Testing Coordinator. Quinton was nominated for the 2021 William P. Foster Community Service Award, an award that is "given to band directors who provide strong music education experiences for their students and a positive impact on their school and community".  In addition to his duties at Lucas, in December 2021, Quinton was also named the Assistant Director of Band at the oldest HBCU in the South, Shaw University. He works as the Assistant Director to Mr. Andrae King, the Director of the Shaw University "Platinum Sound" Marching Band.  Quinton serves as the Director of the "Platinum Sound" Pep Band and assist with the concert band as well.  He was recently named Adjunct Professor of Music for the 2023-2024 School Year.

# RICARDO DAVIS

# CHOCOLATE THUNDER
## The World Famed Tiger Marching Band Drumline
## Thunder Fall 2000

### Ricardo Davis

### Grambling State University

As I reminisce about the good times, I've had being a part of the World Famed Tiger Marching Band, I think of the long lasting memories that I have loved and cherished until this day. I vividly remember going into the band room called "Dunbar." It was the building that contained and held many of the practices. Upon walking in, the Tiger on the wall immediately caught my attention. This image was a large Tiger face which no matter where you walked or sat, the eyes of that tiger seemed to follow you. This Tiger had been used as a method to ensure that you sat up straight, and stared straight ahead during practice. I had this overwhelming feeling of excitement and power. Here I was at Grambling State University, the school known to have the "Best Band in The Land," and I was now a part of it. Walking into the band room and meeting my brother and sisters for the first time, who would have known the journey we were about to embark on. At this time not realizing the bond that we were creating and forging at that very moment was a lifelong friendship that will be a part of me always.

Freshmen Band Camp had begun on August 1st and it lasted throughout the month. I remember we were reminded of how we were now a part of an illustrious tradition and that the egos of who was the best incoming freshmen had to cease. Still thinking I was the best, I heard one of the drill instructors scream out "GET AT ATTENTION NOW, THIS AIN'T SOUTHERN!" My crab brothers and I snapped to attention, standing perfectly still only using our peripheral vision to see what was happening and listening to see if someone was going to get yelled at. I let out an abrupt "YES SIR."

Trying not to smile or show any emotions on my face, I was excited because I knew this was the place for me. While knowing that I was gifted, talented and wanting to become better, I had the drive and determination to become the best. This had been my most sincere dream since that day in high school. One of my mentors, Fred Sanders, who had also played snare drum for the World Famed, took me to Grambling State University to introduce me to my future University and members of the drumline while I was a high school student. As band camp continued, we were taught traditional marching and funk cadences, dance routines, calisthenics, as well as learned countless cadences and solos. When we were released, my crab brothers and I would meet up in my dorm room and talk about how excited we all were to be a part of the World Famed, and challenge each other with what we had learned. My crab brother and good friend still to this very day, Shinderick Washington, asked me "WHAT DOES CRAB mean?" I told him that I really wasn't sure, but it couldn't be too bad, because we were all called that, even when we did nothing wrong. We all laughed about it later on because we found out by our big brother Jason Keys that CRAB is an acronym which means Currently Recruited Active Bandsmen. My crab brothers and I had effectively become brothers, we walked the campus together, we knew about each other's parents, siblings, girlfriends, even favorite foods. During this time, I was nominated Crab kickoff man. This meant that as the leader of the freshmen percussionists, I was responsible for playing and starting the songs and doing numerous other things for the band. I excelled and continued to work on being the best.

I was enjoying myself. I was actually hype that we were waking up reporting at 4 am. That let me know how serious it was. While everyone else was sleeping, we were practicing and getting it in.  The days were counting down to our first game of the season which was a home game. Against one of our rivals in the SWAC, Alcorn. I had no issues of being nervous as many of my crab brothers and sisters were pretty nervous in regards to the first game quickly approaching.

Something was about to happen that would soon erase the doubt and nervousness of my crab brothers and sisters. I had been consistently impressing my drill sergeants, as well as the upperclassmen leaders. I quickly understood what this was really all about. It was about falling in line, about consistently doing what needed to be done and understanding the bigger picture.

It was supposed to be viewed as a boot camp. What we were learning were the tools of the trade to represent the university to the best of our abilities and this ended in us being recognized as an elite marching machine. This is how I saw it when I looked at how everything was about timing down to the letter. We would continue hearing from the upperclassmen "5 more days and those horses will be here!!!" Now this, I understood. The upperclassmen were returning the world famed needed soldiers. Soldiers ready for battle, ready to enter the arena with all their powers at the ready. The upperclassmen were getting ready to return and this is what many of my crab brothers and sisters were afraid of for some reason. I was ready to be a part of this much larger band. I had convinced myself that I would be the very best soldier. That was my mission, to be an asset. The upperclassmen had finally returned and while at the evening practice, something was about to happen that was going to shape who I was and what I was capable of.

The evening practice started and we always were at the band room prior to the start of practice. This was our lives now. To be punctual and be on time. While the sun was going down, at the very front of Dunbar I heard in a very loud voice from Eddie Brown aka PHAT PAT, "Which one of you crabs is TURK?" I looked up nervously assessing the situation and said "I am." He then said to me, "I am hearing you think you are the best crab, and a big shot!" I replied "No I don't." At this moment I noticed that it looked like a school yard fight and a challenger was presented to me to battle me, to see how good I really was. I had battled so much in high school that this was actually a comfort zone for me. Phat yelled out "I got money on my boy for a challenge!" At this moment I heard a voice from behind me that was clear. It was Michael Williams. Michael was an upperclassman and in the leadership lab to be percussion section leader. He was also from my high school and knew what I was capable of. He had taught me many things while in high school. I quickly played a run to set the tone. I made sure that it was clear and concise but slow enough for me to dissect the challengers playing style and technique. This way I could know what type of beats/rhythms to challenge him with. He played back and I noticed that he wasn't using his fingers to play certain things I had played. This let me know what to play and to attack. At that moment, not realizing it, I said "WELL THIS IS OVER." I played the passage with all the speed that I had and it worked. Everyone was quiet. I looked up and noticed a look of shock on some of the upperclassmen faces. But I also noticed that the drill sets as well as the upperclassmen leaders were smirking and smiling. One stated "All really don't know, that boy really is raw!" At that moment my work was done. I looked and saw a very familiar face watching as this transpired. Doc T had made his way through the crowd and was watching. When I made eye contact, I was not sure if I was in trouble, he smiled. Later that night I was asked by the upperclassmen if I knew any funk trains. I told them "Yes I do." Phat asked me "Which ones do you know?" I replied, "All of them." To which he laughed and said "You are very cocky aren't you?" I replied as I had replied before, very short "No I'm not." Let's just say when I performed, I left nothing to chance. This footage is actually on YouTube still as well as in our BICENTENNIAL documentary for the university. I was chosen as one of two freshmen to be interviewed to represent the World Famed for the Bicentennial. Myself and my crab sister who was actually from Hong Kong.

During my time with the World Famed I was traveling and playing so much that it was just all too new and unreal to me. We were treated like celebrities everywhere we went. One time we were practicing and Doc T (Dr. Edwin Thomas) came out and told us we were shooting a commercial for ESPN to which the upperclassmen yelled out "Crabs don't do commercials in unison!" I wasn't upset at all as I I was just happy to be there. Doc T tapped me on my shoulder and told me to wait for a moment. I did and he then informed me that I would be in the commercial. My fondest memories are of him and how much he cared for us.

After leaving Grambling State University and starting my profession, I started volunteering with Huntington High School in Shreveport, Louisiana. I was there teaching and training the young men and women to be the very best and this very same drumline in Louisiana is a household name. The nickname I gave them is "THE GODS" Phi Gods of War drumline. Over the years we won so many first-place battles and all the while I was sending material that I created to Grambling State University. Almost nine years after creating this unique and creative drumline, while still in high school, they are requested all over as special guests to play and entertain for crowds in many different venues. I was tapped in 2019 to become a percussion instructor at Grambling State University by Dr. Nikole Roebuck, current head band director of the World Famed. I am currently still at Grambling State continuing the tradition of winning that Dr. Thomas installed in me all those decades ago. Life really does come around full circle to those that are committed.

## About Ricardo Davis

Mr. Ricardo Davis is from Shreveport, Louisiana. He fell in love with band at the age of six and remembers going to a football game with my mother to watch my oldest brother Paul perform. He was the Tuba section leader at Fair Park High School. Ricardo was amazed and knew that he wanted to be in a band. Since there weren't any instrument at his home, he would go out in the backyard and pretend to be in a band. He would beat on our barbecue pit with sticks that he found on the ground. Mr. Davis' brother saw that he was passionate and he introduced him to his friend Troy. Troy played snare drum for Texas Southern University marching band. At the age of eleven, Ricardo excitedly joined the middle school band at Bethune Middle School. Even though he wanted to learn how to play other instruments as well, he had his heart set on playing the drums. His band director, Mr. Paul Tinker stated that Ricardo needed a pair of drum sticks and the RuBank Elementary Method Drum book by Paul Yoder. He excelled at learning to read percussion music and was first chair in the District Honor Band.

The first song Mr. Davis learned to play was *March of the Phantom Brigade.* In high school, he was finally about to realize his dream by joining the legendary Fair Park High School Marching Band under the direction of Mr. Cleveland R. White. Not only was this his dream, but he was following in the footsteps of his oldest brother Paul, whom he looked up to. Even though he still had a lot of learning to do. Mr. White asked him to be his percussion section leader. He stated that Ricardo was talented and very creative. A couple of the upper and former classmates Frederick Sanders and Fred Taylor coached him after school and after practice, helping him to better his craft. During his junior year of high school, he visited Grambling State University campus. The Dunbar band room is where he met the whole drum line and had a chance to watch them rehearse. He knew right then and there that this was the HBCU he wanted to attend.

During Ricardo's senior year, he auditioned for scholarships and received full scholarships to Alcorn State University, University of Arkansas Pine Bluff and Texas Southern University. He also received scholarships to Jackson State University and Southern University. He received a P1 scholarship to Grambling State University by his Maestro Doctor Edwin Thomas better known as Doc T. When he graduated from Fair Park High school, he enrolled as a freshman at Grambling State University and Majored in Computer Science. Being a member of the best drumline. The World Famed Tiger Marching Band was a blessing in itself. Mr. Davis has elevated his skills and creativity beyond measures. He is thankful to YHWH for allowing him to have had this experience. In 2011-2018, he was the percussion instructor for Huntington High School in Shreveport, Louisiana. He founded the legendary "Gods of War Drum line" (GPHIW), where they were highly ranked and won countless first place trophies. The Most High, YHWH, have blessed many young men and women to attend Universities with percussion scholarships. Ricardo is currently the  percussion instructor at Grambling State University, where he had started his collegiate percussion training to be the very best.

# MYLES TILFORD

# "Be Present, Not Perfect"
## Myles Tilford
### Southern University A&M College

When most people describe their experiences being in a HBCU band you often hear about how long the practice schedules are, the time spent preparing for a single performance, or the lack of time for a social life. However, the concept of time that is often overlooked are those small windows of moments where you have nothing else to do in the band room except sit down and think. I can vividly remember conversations I've had in my head, while music was being dissected for hours, on what my life would potentially be like when my time in the Southern University Human Jukebox had ended. Never would I have imagined that my surface level aspirations would manifest into becoming my passion filled reality and I owe that all to the best band in the land.

My love for the Human Jukebox started back when I was in the 6th grade. My family and I went to the Bayou Classic that year in 2008 and as much as I've seen the band in the past, it was something about that year that initiated my desire towards marching in the band. My dad, Wendel Tilford Jr. is a fellow former member of the band, educator, and active musician. His connection with the band allowed me to meet Dr. Isaac Greggs in high school, attend multiple high school band camps at Southern, and witness numerous of his former band students transform into collegiate musicians. These encounters assisted in inspiring me to attend Southern University and stepping into HBCU band culture.

My story of becoming a Juke started how I often live life today which is, my own level of chaos. As much as I like to spend my free time thinking, that also leads to unwarranted invitations for overthinking. My audition for the band had so many external factors that clouded my judgment for how I wanted it to go. Thanks to my amazing hometown of Houston, TX, my dad and I were stuck in traffic that caused me to be an hour late to when the auditions were going to end. As I arrived at the audition site of Westbury High School, it was painfully obvious that I was the last one to audition for the day. Luckily, my dad was with me to be my support system and to be my buffer to get in the building. I knew that his presence was going to allow me to get my foot in the door to still audition, but I was going to have to depend on my musicianship to secure my place. When it was time for me to begin my audition, I had every director in the program present to hear me play my trumpet. With being late still on my mind, having a make-or-break moment present in my face, and knowing that the last 4 measures of my prepared piece was going to kick my tail, I was having full on sensory overload. I flew through playing my scales and the sight-reading portion, but psyched myself out when it was time for the prepared piece. Between me stopping and starting over at every single mistake I made while playing my piece, I had to actively fight off my nerves. I was so nervous after my audition that I completely overlooked Mr. Haymer informing me that I made the band. It took two weeks until I received a call from the Lawerence E. Jackson, II Foundation informing me that I received a musician scholarship for it to finally hit me that my hard work had succeeded.

My freshman year, in hindsight, was an intense season for personal growth. Due to everything I had to face being a freshman in college, I learned the importance of self-discipline and trusting my intuition in an unfamiliar environment. I spent that first year embracing the lifestyle change that the band provided for me and envisioning how I wanted to evolve as my years went by. Honestly my fondest memory of my freshman year was coming home after the season was over and comparing my band stories with my dad. I loved being part of the band era where social media was still emerging and that our media team was phenomenal at capturing every moment during the season. I was thankful to have visual representation of my highlights for the season and to be able to share that with my main Juke inspiration meant a lot to me.

My sophomore year in the band is what changed the game for me completely as I discovered new talents within myself. My favorite moments in the band room were when it was time for us to practice the dance routine for our halftime performances because it was the only time I could move freely. In the back of my mind freshman year, I was anticipating the opportunity to be part of the Super 7, but the moment never presented itself. My 2nd year in the band I didn't want to intentionally blend in with my class like I did the year prior. My crab siblings in my section were incredible trumpet players and with it being over 26 of us, I wanted a domain in the band that I could dominate and stand out the most in. When it was announced that there were auditions being held during practice to be in the Notorious 9 and perform in front of the band at homecoming, I jumped at the chance. When I looked around at everyone participating in the auditions, the room mainly consisted of individuals that were already part of the dance routine committee. I knew that I was going to have to outperform everyone to be seen, being that I spent the majority of my time hiding in the band room and rotating the same three people I talked to on a daily basis. Unlike other times when my anxiety would get the best of me at practice, I was confident that I was going to eat up my audition with ease. The audition consisted of us performing two dance routines in front of the Fabulous Dancing Dolls, as they were the judges. When it was time for my audition group to perform, I purposely placed myself in the middle of the dance formation and the rest is history. I've always known I could dance, but I wasn't aware of the magnitude of my ability. Moving into my Junior year in the band, I joined the dance routine committee and by the time my senior year came around, I was teaching the routines to the entire band. I was very proud to say that I was able to contribute to the band program and that my contribution is forever displayed on the internet.

When times were hard and college life seemed to be overwhelming, I asked myself early on what my purpose was for being in the band. As time went on, I discovered that I loved that adrenaline feeling I would get when I performed. Anytime there was a small band group performance, a selected group, pep band, or anything else that allowed me extra time to perform, I was there. As graduation approached, I told myself that I needed to do something in my career that would allow me to not lose that adrenaline feeling that I loved. That's the moment I knew that I wanted to pursue a career in entertainment. The summer before my senior year in the band, I was approached to sign with a local talent/modeling agency in Houston. I didn't think much of it until the week of graduation I had a conversation with Mr. Simmons on what were my plans post grad. After that encounter, I contacted the agency and had a casting call scheduled the next day after graduation. Since being signed with my agency, I've danced in music videos, have been featured in magazines, commercials, films, and have done numerous print work. The work ethic, discipline, and experience that I've gained while being in the Human Jukebox has carried over tremendously in my professional career. I came into the band as a reserved kid who didn't want any attention thrown his way, but my dreams for myself were bigger than my comfortability. I've left the band very confident in what I can produce out into the world and most importantly, in myself.

## About Myles Tilford

Myles Tilford, originally born in Baton Rouge, LA, is a current native of Houston, TX. During his matriculation at Southern University A&M College, where he received his Bachelor of Science in Psychology (Spring 2019), Mr. Tilford participated in a multitude of organizations that helped shape his colligate experience. Mr. Tilford is a former president of Psi Chi, the International Honor Society in Psychology, former member of the Southern University Gospel Choir, the Colligate 100 of Southern University, Jaguar Ambassador, and proud 4-year member of the Southern University Human Jukebox. Mr. Tilford marched in the Southern University Human Jukebox from Fall 2015 to Spring 2019 where he played the trumpet. After graduating from Southern University, Mr. Tilford has transitioned into becoming a mental health professional, model, actor, dancer, songwriter, and now author. Mr. Tilford is currently employed at a mental health agency in Houston, TX where he is a Service Coordinator providing individuals with mental disabilities services that help to improve the quality of their life. Mr. Tilford is a signed talent/model with the Neal Hamil Agency where some of his featured work includes, print work for Target, Nike, & LGI Homes, as well as commercials for State Farm, UPS, and Virtuix. As his career continues to progress, Myles Tilford is thankful for his time in the Southern University Human Jukebox for inspiring him to reach further than he could've ever anticipated.

# APRIL SHELL

# Love, Life, and Leadership

**April Shell**

**South Carolina State University**

"Whistle, two, three, four, up two kick step!" is the famous call and response which depicts the relationship between a drum major and her band. Engaging with the Marching 101 Band in this manner for the first time in Oliver C. Dawson Stadium was the highlight of my senior year at South Carolina State University. Before I had the awesome privilege of becoming a Bulldog, I was a proud Raider at W. J. Keenan High School, and that is where it all started. I can vividly remember one sunny day in May, after a long day at school, and musical sectionals were happening everywhere. They were happening in the dugouts, on the gridiron, up the hill towards the tennis course, and many other areas that could hold an entire instrument section. Yes, it was May and it was time to select the leadership positions for the band. While the music was playing everywhere, I was coming from a meeting and had a dress on that day, which was rare for me, and for some reason I decided not to change before I went to the band field. W.E. Lyles, a graduate of South Carolina State University, and our band director at the time, called us over to the middle of the field and stated that it was time for those who wanted to try out for drum major to come forward. I had no intentions of trying out, but one of my dearest friends, and flute section member told me she was going for it. So, I said, "Ok, I'll go out too!" We did everything together along with a few others that went to middle school with us; and this was no different. It was that year I was chosen as drum major and served in that capacity both my junior and senior year and that was the beginning of things I didn't know were coming.

During my senior year in high school, my friends and I were selecting colleges to apply for, but there was only one choice and no need for me to look any further than my S-C-S-U! I understood from an early age what my parents had planned for me and I knew that their finances were not going anywhere else; and that was just fine with me because I had enjoyed traveling to Orangeburg, SC as a child for as long as I could remember and I loved it! One thing I couldn't wait for each time was the half-time show and the Marching 101! So, of course, I didn't look any further and I applied to South Carolina State in the field of Math Education and excitedly awaited for my journey as a Bulldog to begin. The sights and sounds of the crowd roaring, the inspiring cheerleaders, our most friendly bulldog Mascot, the sounds of the opposing bands, and "Get Up for the Bulldogs, everybody get up!", football games at an HBCU are unlike any other. The fans eagerly await halftime so that they can enjoy the friendly musical banter between bands. On the field, it becomes a different type of battle when the football players move to their respective locker rooms. The bands were ready, the cheerleaders were ready, and everyone else would sit patiently waiting for the moment when the band announcers would introduce each band. Fans are eager to see who will win bragging rights until they battle again. Bandsmen, on the other hand, eagerly anticipate the beloved 5th Quarter when the bands of the two opposing schools battle each other for bragging rights to the best musical performance. The 5th Quarter in the world of HBCU football takes place after the game for about 20-30 minutes and just happens to be one of my favorite moments when rival bands are there to perform against us. "Hey, I love my HBCU, I love my HBCU, I love my HBCU, SCSU, SCSU" in my Carolina Anthem voice!

The summer before I left for campus, I went to Carowinds with some friends and purchased a keychain that said, Marching 101. I was in, or so I thought. As I finished at the Kiosk, I saw a group of guys with their Marching 101 band, known as the Bongo Brothers, who I later found out were the members of the percussion section of the band. I ran up to them and said, "Hey, I'm going to be a member of the Marching 101!" One of them said, "slow it down, and please don't wear it. You will have to wait until you complete an entire marching band season before you can wear any Marching 101 paraphernalia, except for performing of course." I was heartbroken, but respected the culture I was about to embark upon. They told me that they would be at band camp in a few months and to be sure to remind them of who I was. They would later become great friends of mine as I spent all four years of college in the band. With twists and turns along with the freshman 15, I strived to be a successful student as well as one for service. I became a member of Tau Beta Sigma, National Honorary Band Sorority as well as a member of Delta Sigma Theta Sorority, Inc. With both sororities being service oriented I gained insight on what it means to be a servant leader and how impactful it can be for others. In a complete full circle moment, at the end of my junior year I decided to go back to Keenan High School to the Jazz Band Show; an annual show with a mix of talents and abilities of members of the band. I went backstage to see Mr. Lyles. Near the end of our conversation, he said, "You know there has never been a female drum major for the Marching 101." I turned and looked at him with wide-eyes and said, "So, what are you suggesting? Do you think that I could actually become the first female?" He said in so many words that God speaks to him so that he can plant seeds in others. That night I started thinking and praying about this possibility. I then consulted several people about it including my parents and close friends. Needless to say, I could not get the thought of it out of my head and later concluded that since I had experience in high school, "Why not try!" In the spring of 1997 during spring drills, in front of the entire band, I stood up and announced that I was trying out for drum major. The entire band roared and applauded my bulldog tenacity and the rest is history.

My drum major experiences taught me how to be patient, as well as how to analyze and read the room. It taught me how to discern and deliver the pace, tone and direction of a command. I learned how to be courageous, and gained tools for inner strength, as well as the ability to persevere through any obstacle. Currently, as a Principal I have used these same leadership skills to lead, direct and guide others. In comparison to the drum major position, the principal is the conductor of the school, leading sections of the building at any given moment. Section leaders lead their department and strive to align the standards in perfect harmony known as instructional strategies so that we can all reach the finale, which is student success. As John Maxwell states, "A leader is one who knows the way, goes the way and shows the way," and the HBCU Band experience has certainly influenced me in this effort in education for 25 years. I could not have done this without God, because it is my belief that, "I can do all things through Christ who strengthens me." Without the encouragement of Willie E. Lyles, the support of my parents, friends and fellow band members, as well as the collective belief of the late Ronald J. Sergeant and the entire staff of the Marching 101 Band in the late 90's, none of this would have been possible. They all had faith in me so that I could fulfill my destiny as the first female drum major of the Marching 101 Band. This is written in the history books at SCSU for all to see and it will also be a part of my legacy forever.

# About April Shell

April Nicole Shell is the proud Principal of Summit Parkway Middle School in Columbia, SC, where she has served in this role since 2017. For the past 25 years, she has been passionate about education because she would like to continue to be an agent of change. Driven by inspiring and motivating others she takes pride in providing the best culture and environment for her school. As an Instructional Leader her goals are to increase student achievement and propel the professional growth of the faculty and staff. In 2023, her school's magnet programs received national certification by the Magnet Schools of America. In 2010, she was awarded the "Excellence in Management" Award by the Richland School District Two Superintendent.

She has previously served in Richland Two as a math teacher, assistant administrator, assistant principal, and behavior interventionist. Upon graduating, she began her teaching career in 1998 in Richland School District One as a math teacher at W. G. Sanders Middle School, where in 2000-2001 she was named "Teacher of the Year" by her colleagues and awarded the "Who's Who Award Among Teachers".

April holds a Bachelor of Science Degree in Mathematics Education from South Carolina State University where she graduated with honors. She also obtained a Master of Education Degree in Education Administration from the University of South Carolina. April has been recognized for her extraordinary commitment to her personal development by completing leadership programs developed by the State Department of South Carolina and the South Carolina Association of School Administrators.

As a student at South Carolina State University, April dedicated four years to the marching band, symphonic band and jazz band. She mastered the flute, piccolo, piano, and keyboard. In1997, she was selected to be the first female drum major of the SC State Marching 101 Band. This was her destined legacy as she later inspired three additional females to lead and direct the marching band. In 1998, April received the highest honor when was inducted in the SC State University Jazz Band Hall of Fame. April has also received various music awards and recognitions, such as Most Effective Leader, Most Dedicated, Most Outstanding Freshman, Best All Around, Best Female Dancer, and Most Spirited Female, Most Outstanding Jazz Band Sophomore & Junior, and Who's Who Among Colleges and Universities.

She is the proud daughter of Donnie and Paulette Shell and serves on the board of the Donnie Shell Scholarship Foundation. She is a member of Delta Sigma Theta Sorority, Inc. and Tau Beta Sigma National Honorary Band Sorority, Inc. Outside of professional interest, April is an avid reader, writer and musician. She is a licensed health and life coach and loves to inspire others to learn more about physical fitness and nutrition. Her favorite scripture is, Philippians 4:13, "I can do all things through Christ who strengthens me."

# DR. TIA N. LOCKE-SIMMONS

# Lifelong Lesson and Drum Love

Dr. Tia N. Locke-Simmons

Prairie View A&M University

I was probably born with a love for the band. I grew up in a home that was always filled with music…not just Saturday morning chores music…every day we played music. I can trace the feelings of music vibrating in my soul back to all things Motown, Johnny Guitar Watson, Chaka Khan, Earth, Wind, and Fire, The Emotions, Teddy Pendergrass, Marvin Gaye, Aretha Franklin, and Wes Montgomery… you get the picture.  What really gets me? It's always drums for me! A love for great music paired with years of dance training cemented this love for me. I trained under the dance leadership of Madame Tou Braudy Whittington, Etta Jamison, Doris Zanders, and even the great Pearl Primus while I was in the Alvin Ailey Intensive Program! I studied every dance discipline but it is my study of African Dance that ties me back to the drums. The funny thing is that Herbie Mann, the American Jazz Flutist, still reigns supreme in my drum-love for his piece *Bird in a Silver Cage*. He made that flute feel like drums in my body. You know the feeling when music penetrates your body and forces movement…dance!

In middle school, I signed up for band just for the opportunity to play the drums. Mr. Dean Hill, my band teacher at O. W. Holmes in Dallas, gave me a shot. I was horrible but he saw my heart and convinced me that the flute could be my friend. I learned to play the flute so I could be near drums during the school day. By the time I made it to high school, I was dancing in front of the band. It was natural that I would become a Black Fox and march in front of the Prairie View A & M Marching Storm. The percussion section was known as The Box. I lived for The Box and could be found nearby so I could feel the base in my chest. Let me share what is beyond the excitement of band, the glittered heels we marched in, the feeling in the air when you saw us coming, and the precision of the messaging in the strategic formations on the field.

You have to understand that when I enrolled in Prairie View, the first thing my daddy said to me was "You better not be a Black Fox! I will come to get you off the field." Please also know that I believed him and that I auditioned to be a Black Fox at the earliest possible opportunity. Dr. Margarette Penn Sherrod was the director of the Black Foxes, as well as the founder. The late George Edwards directed the band. The expectation from both was excellence, nothing less and always room for more excellence. What I found, and continue to carry in my professional life are these tenets:

- Save it for the field.

- Whatever you do must be done with class.

- Work hard. Make it look easy. The audience came to see you.

*Save it for the field.*
–PROFESSOR GEORGE EDWARDS AKA PROF

We were the rivaled SWAC band. Anytime we have a big game, the opposing team's band would have plenty to say…word of mouth. We had beepers then so there was no texting or Twitter. These noise talking sessions would erupt into unnecessary occurrences for some schools. Not ours. Prof would not allow it. He would have sat a drum major on the sideline for it even moments before the halftime performance. When other bands engaged us in this behavior, Prof's firm guidance to us was, "Save it for the field."

Throughout my professional career, I have been in environments where I was the only female, or only African American, or the youngest, or most inexperienced. I have often been the recipient of side-eyes, racial slurs, and invisibility treatment. You can choose to respond and defend. Or, you can save it for the field…meaning you have a choice for how you use your energy. You can use it to defend something that is truly indefensible, people's chosen perceptions; or, you can get busy being the best you can possibly be and leave a stellar performance on the field. Believe me, your work will speak louder than any words you use in an attempt to get others to understand what they really do not want to understand.

Agreed, Prof Edwards was our band director. He was responsible for teaching and arranging music, organizing formations for the field, and ensuring we moved as one band with one sound. The reality of an HBCU band is that it is far more than the music and performances. An HBCU band is filled with life lessons and life-long relationships. Whatever arises on your path…and things will arise…save it for the field!

*Whatever you do must be done with class.*
*Work hard. Make it look easy.*
*The audience came to see you.*
– DR. MARGARET PENN SHERROD

As Black Foxes, we were seen in leotards and tights. To the naked eye, we may have seemed underdressed with every curve on display. We moved as one and looked as one. Our faces were colored in stage makeup and red lipstick such that you could see our smiles from the seats on the last row, at the top of the stadium. It was intentional. To protect the integrity of our on-field attire, Dr. Sherrod maintained extremely high expectations for the manner in which we carried ourselves in all other places. In addition to Prof and Dr. Sherrod's expectations that we matriculate and graduate; Dr. Sherrod had non-negotiables: *Whatever you do must be done with class, and Work hard. Make it look easy. The audience came to see you.*

Dr. Sherrod was absolutely responsible for leading us as a dance troupe, vetting choreography and costumes, verifying grades, and ensuring we were field-ready. What was never spoken but always understood is that Dr Sherrod was also responsible for ushering us into womanhood. We were fresh out of our high school, thought we were grown, and needed guidance on the transition into womanhood that was unknowingly before us. The clearly communicated expectations were, do it with class and make it look easy.

I can recall a performance at Texas A & M where Dr. Sherrod checked our pregame wardrobe and had a love-filled but firm coaching conversation about attire. We were assured that our intended brand was represented by our attire choices, bearing in mind that the greater community sees us (and remembers) in form-fitting minimal costumes. At this same game, I wanted to wear my new pink lip gloss. It was super cute. Dr. Sherrod quickly redirected me explaining that the person in the seat furthest from the field deserved to see my smile. Field makeup was required and every person in the audience deserved the same experience. And, yes! Still at the same game, it was freezing cold. We were debuting a new white costume with metallic gold appliques and tank top shoulder straps. Oh, how we trembled. Dr. Sherrod, again, advised that we were performers. The audience came to see us. She always made sure we knew when we needed to improve and never let an opportunity pass to remind us that we were dynamic, that there was someone in the audience who wanted to be where we were. "Make it look easy."

To whom much is given, much is required. I never take what is entrusted to me for granted. When I am feeling weary about what is before me, I think of Dr. Sherrod, put my shoulders back and step forward knowing that someone else wants to be where I am, everyone watching deserves my best performance, work hard and present the product with ease.

I still live for the percussion section of the Marching Storm and stand forever grateful for the relationships and life-long lessons that only come from having been a part of an HBCU band. The bond is serious.

# About Dr. Tia N. Locke-Simmons

In a society vastly shaped by ideals of prominence and opulent pursuits; it is who we are at our core, that defines life's true elucidation. Helping professionals' harness that sentiment authentically, is the compassionate professional, Dr. Tia N. Locke-Simmons.

Tia is a three-time Amazon International Best-Selling Author, speaker, pedagogic guru, and the originator and founder of global inHERprises; a multidimensional platform centered around the fundamental practice of inner healing, cognitive evolvement, and self-actualization, in the lives of women. Having spent more than two decades as a premier educator, behavioral specialist, and in various roles of leadership; Tia infuses the synergy and erudition acquired in her career, with an authentic love for seeing women become their best selves.

**Her mantra is simple: she wants to help others focus on the inner work to reach outward manifestations.**

Tia N. Locke-Simmons combines an outstanding career with a sincere regard for higher learning, achievement, and community involvement. She holds a **BA** in **Psychology**, an **M.Ed.** in **Educational Leadership**, and an **Ed.D.** in **Educational Leadership** in December 2021. She has received two certificates, **Higher Education Teaching and Learning and Urban School Leadership**, from **Harvard University**. Her expertise is counted as one of the most trusted in her field, as she is certified as a Texas superintendent, administrator, and generic special education teacher. Tia has been recognized for her outstanding contributions in leadership, serves on several boards and organizations, and has been gainfully awarded for her trailblazing approach, to both social and communal needs. She was selected as a Region IV Aspiring

Superintendents Cohort, recognized as Texas Association of Gifted and Talented Administrator of the Year, and as an Emerging Leader. As a high school executive principal, she led her campus to be a recipient of the U.S. News and World Report Recognition for Best High Schools in America. She has received Trailblazer of the Year, Principal of the Year, and Yellow Rose Civic Award, and many more.

She is a proud member of Delta Sigma Theta Sorority, Incorporated and is a Past President of Houston Alumnae Chapter of Delta Sigma Theta Sorority, Incorporated. Tia is also a founding member of the Houston Metropolitan Area Section of the National Council of Negro Women, and a Life Member of the NAACP, and many more - a true testament of her commitment to service, human excellence, and the empowerment and solace of women.

Tia attests that it is God, and His handiwork in the lives of people, that inspires her the most and is the perpetual reason she is committed to helping others manifest their best in life. When Tia isn't out helping the global community become its best, she is an asset to her local community and a loving member of her family and friendship circles.

# HEPSTON H. HENRY II

# An Appetite for Music
## Hepston H. Henry II
## Norfolk State University

I love music. There was never a time where it was not playing in my house. Reggae, Calypso, gospel, R&B, and hip-hop (when I could sneak and listen to it). My grandfather was an amazing musician who could play anything, but couldn't read a lick of music! I thought this was the coolest thing ever as a kid. He was a police officer by day, and a musician by moonlight. And he was never late for work! Ira A. Samuel, Sr. was known on St. Croix and throughout the Virgin Islands for playing with many bands. I wanted to be *That* guy.

I joined band in 6th grade playing the alto saxophone. I realized quickly that I despised practicing. I still did it though. I switched to tenor sax my sophomore year of high school because my band director needed another one for the jazz band. Still, I hated practicing. I became drum major my junior year, which gave me an excuse to be off of my horn. This was my thought process. Terrible. It carried into college as I was a Music Education turned Music Media major. Don't get me wrong, I was still a good player, but more hours in the practice room, and I could've been Great! My focus was more on music production and engineering. Now THIS is what I loved. This was my passion. I would skip class in high school and go down to the studio to learn how to make beats. My best friend was in the class, but my schedule was already full so I couldn't take it. Missing twenty minutes of History wasn't going to hurt. I already had an 'A' in the class.

I could stay up until sunrise making beats with only a honey bun and a bottle of water. I just knew I was going to be the next big sought-after producer from Virginia. Me and my brother. Any genre, any tempo, any style, any key, any rhythm—we did it. So well, in fact, we were signed to a major label; briefly. On top of the world one day, then tumbling down the next. After the terrible business practices and our naiveté, we decided to just stay independent. And it worked out just fine. Those quarterly residual checks aren't as big as they used to be, but I will still gladly take that $2.47! I also arranged music for several high school and college bands. I still produce music to this day, too. I have released several instrumental projects...but it has definitely taken a backseat to my purpose.

While the music was blasting in my house, the sweet aromas of curry goat, stew chicken, red snapper, arroz con pollo, ox tail, and all kinds of soups filled every corner of every room. I loved cooking since I could reach the stove. How could I not??? With all this great food always in the kitchen, it was best I learned how to make it! Cooking was also a necessity in my household. Basic life skills were taught at a young age. I learned quickly that this was not a common practice in other families. Fast forward to my years at NSU; my roommates, frat brothers, sorors, and friends always came by my apartment for food. My mom and sister would come periodically to cook for us and leave some of her seasoning. We used that stuff on *everything* growing up. I used to just give away the extra to them because I knew my mom had a few mason jars at home. I would cook for all of my friends too. We all knew how to cook, and would frequently share meals. Even after college, I would go on to cook for friends. I went to my frat brother's apartment one time to cook some curry chicken for a group of friends. We said our grace, and sat down to eat. I looked around, and everyone's face was down at their plates. The only sound in the whole room was forks hitting the plate. I looked around and nodded, taking in that moment.

"Aye, we're having a little get-together, you coming through and cooking something?"

"Hep you got some more of your mama seasoning?"

"Yo, you should sell this stuff!"

I heard these questions so often, that it finally started to resonate. So, finally in 2019 I decided to do just that. I started off with just the All-purpose blend, since that was all I planned to do. Some people suggested a salt free version and one with no Cayenne pepper. I then added Jerk, then Spicy garlic. I knew I didn't want to get too overzealous. But I also knew that I didn't want to limit my creativity either.

Then the pandemic hit. Everyone was at home, however, they were cooking more. Business was booming! I even got more creative and branched out to make more blends. Starting from just a suggestion, I have now created almost 30 different blends, with more to come. I love this. Everything is low sodium, gluten free, vegan friendly, and contains no additives or preservatives. I needed to do this. WE needed me to do this. This is my happy place. Too many ailments and diseases come from a poor diet or just poor nutrition overall. The spices you see on the shelf in grocery stores are packed full of ingredients that are simply there to dilute or to extend their shelf life. I started reading labels more and more. Most of that stuff people can't even pronounce. Even if they can, do they know what it is?

On this journey, I've become more in tune with what I put in my body, and I love helping others do the same. Through A.L.L. Seasoning, I express my love for people. I listen to music every single time I'm making my blends late at night in an otherwise quiet house. This is why I'm here. This is my purpose. Food and Music.

## About Hepston H. Henry II

Hepston H. Henry II was born in Queens, NY to West Indian parents. His father is from Jamaica and his mother is from St. Croix. Being raised as an Army brat, Hepston had the opportunity to travel the world, which helped him appreciate many cultures. Little did he know, this would have a major effect on his life. His grandfather was renowned musician Ira Samuel Sr., who gave him his first saxophone. Hepston continued to play the sax through college. His love for band and music led him to join Kappa Kappa Psi National Honorary Band Fraternity, Inc. After graduating cum laude in 2007 with a BA in Music Media, Hepston went on to continue his life in music by managing a recording studio in Virginia Beach, VA. He later started his music production company Frat MuziKK Group with a longtime friend and frat brother. They have worked on several projects for numerous independent and mainstream artists, and have had music licensed film and TV as well.

With music still in his heart, Hepston turned to his other love; food. In a Caribbean household, everyone had to learn *all* the basic life skills, which included cooking. Realizing how tiring it is to be a caterer, he decided to make the seasoning others could use to cook for themselves. In 2019, Mr. Henry launched *A Little Love Seasoning* with the motto "Food tastes better when it's made with A little Love." Starting with just the all-purpose blend his family used growing up, A.L.L. Seasoning has expanded to over 25 blends; all of which are low sodium, vegan friendly, and gluten-free. Too many products contain extra salt, sugars, preservatives, or additives only used for longer shelf life, and to dilute the products. Hepston decided to take matters into his own hands, and provide a bold, flavorful alternative. Mr. Henry has collaborated with several chefs, caterers, and social media influencers. Now in seven stores, Hepston Henry and A.L.L. Seasoning are on a path to be on shelves everywhere.

# RODERICK JEFFERSON

# Exceptionally Rare
## Roderick Jefferson
## Grambling State University

"G S G S G S G S U U U I Thought You Knew" sends chills down and up your spine. It is unexplainable, electric and impressive to say the least. Nothing like the crowd participating in a school chant that you enjoy doing. The crazy thing is becoming a Gramblinite has always been in the cards for me. Being a native of Shreveport, Grambling was the first college band that I witnessed. Witnessing them competing against Alcorn, in the 80's and 90's, in Shreveport at Independence Stadium during the Red River Classic football game was mind-blowing. The pageantry that the band possessed was unmatched because no one could entertain like The World Famed in my eyes. School pride might keep others from stating that verbatim because we did things a little different than most but deep down everyone knew they had to bring their "A Game" when meeting up with The World Famed on the field.

My dad was a Southern University Jag, and he marched in The Human Jukebox on Sousaphone so when I made my decision to attend Grambling, people were shocked. Even though Southern had a couple of games in Shreveport they just did not catch my attention like Grambling did. I respected their brassy sound, but Grambling had that WOW factor on the field which was the most important aspect of a band back then. It was so normal seeing Grambling in Shreveport: from the Red River Classic to the African American History Parade to tv commercials and more. Grambling was the most watched band in America so who would not want to be a part of something great. My senior year in high school sealed the deal. I auditioned with Curtis Willis, the former Director of Bands of Grambling in 1992 in Shreveport at Fair Park High School. Just his presence alone made me excited to be a member of the Tiger Marching Band.

My story is so rare, and some will be shocked but here goes. My first year at Grambling was Fall 1992. The stay was short due to a car accident. I reported to Band Camp on August 1st in 1992 and the camp was not a walk in the park. When I say we exercised, we exercised! We could not run from that Louisiana heat in the Piney Woods of Grambling, Louisiana. The Drill Sergeants were super intense and did not accept just anything. There was a system of grand expectations from the staff to the student leaders and that is why the band performed at such a prominent level.

I distinctly remember during camp getting prepared for Alcorn in 1992. I remember the entire show like it was yesterday: "The Best Things in Life Are Free" by Luther Vandross and Janet Jackson, "Baby, Baby, Baby" by TLC and "Jump, Jump" by Kris Kross. Repeating "Alcorn Trying to Rock but They Can't Rock Like This" just created so much pride because we knew we were about to put it on Alcorn. The second month of school I returned home because of a car accident and afterwards I just could not focus. I was devastated and thought my college and band life was over.

I am the type of person that always finishes what he starts. So, I vowed to return but I returned later than sooner. Even though I went back home, helped my mom, worked, and assisted various Band Directors that led my high school alma mater's band "Woodlawn", I took what I learned at Grambling and that helped me make a significant impact on the Woodlawn High School Band Program. That really showed me what I was put on this earth to do. People always told me that I should go back to Grambling to finish my degree because I was gifted. I planned to but I just wanted to make sure everything at home was going well before I departed again. I recruited many to the band at Grambling and have been since 1992 and I am still doing it to this day. Being a native of Louisiana and only 45 minutes from Grambling it was just natural for me to support

"Da G". I would even take students to Bayou Classic every year to allow them to see for themselves the greatness and the school spirit of Grambling State University. I assisted Woodlawn from 1993-2004 and I knew it was time for me to return to Grambling to complete my degree, now here comes the interesting part.

I returned to Grambling Spring 2004, they coined me "Old School" because of my age and already previously marching at Grambling. Returning to Grambling at age 30 and still being in shape shocked people and to most I still looked like a teen. I contemplated marching again but since I did not complete my marching band career during my first stint at Grambling, I decided to march. Man, this was an interesting experience because for one, I was the oldest member in the band, even though I did not look like it, but it was just my calling. Even though I was older and more mature from when I first attended Grambling, I still complied with all rules and listened because I set the example for others. Once Fall 2004 hit it was really on because I went through band camp once again, crazy thing, it felt like the first time because I was never scared of demanding work. I could still handle the exercises, drilling, attitudes of others and whatever came with being in the band. I played various instruments, many do not know but my first instrument was percussion, I also learned trumpet and French horn in high school. I also played baritone and saxophone.

I decided to stick with the saxophone in the band due to the injury that I received in the wreck cutting muscles that impacted my embouchure. Saxophone was my best fit after the wreck. Man being in the saxophone section in the World Famed was so rewarding because the section had so much pride. No one could out march, nor outplay the section because everyone held everyone else accountable. When you are a part of a section that won "section of the year" multiple times while you marched, that showed the section itself has a system. I formed so many bonds in the section. Me and my saxophone brothers and sisters never had dull moments. We always were with each other: either off campus at one of my saxophone sisters' or brothers' apartments in Ruston, Louisiana or me and my brothers would chill in my room in Attucks Hall. We are tight and everyone knows that.

Once I got acclimated back to the band my next goal was pledging Kappa Kappa Psi and I completed that journey in Spring 2005. Man, I can draft a book about this experience by itself, but I will be brief this time. While embarking on the Kappa Kappa Psi process, me and my line brothers lived in the library to study. To be chosen was a blessing because that means others saw you as a leader and Kappa Kappa Psi National Honorary Band Fraternity were the leaders of The Grambling State University World Famed Tiger Marching Band. After I completed the journey, I became an active student arranger for the band. Sometimes our field shows consisted of just my arrangements, other than the precision drills which were usually concert marches. I enjoyed arranging for the band and being on the dance committee. I knew I had to be a part of the committee always because I grew up on Grambling and knew Grambling like the back of my hand, so I wanted to make sure The World Famed continued the mystique it possessed of pageantry.

In 2007 when I became the Student Conductor of the band, I was so excited because I knew it was my chance to really display my talents. I was fortunate that Dr. Pannell, Director of Bands, really trusted me. He allowed me to hold rehearsals and even teach my arrangements, which has helped mold me to this day. I remember our first game in 2007, it was in Lorman, Mississippi against Alcorn. We made it in the stadium before Alcorn. We were wondering, "where is Alcorn?" We finally heard drums and seen purple and gold marching into the stadium and then we crunk up "Torture" by The Jacksons. Their crowd went wild and could not believe it because Grambling was looked at as strictly a field band and was not known to throw the first blow in the stands. The band was on point the entire game. During halftime we stole their crowd when we performed the dance to Soulja Boy's "CRANK THAT" and the Cupid Shuffle. When the Band Directors came out and did the shuffle the band received a ROAR of APPLAUSE, everyone was on their feet as we marched out and continued to applaud even after we played the last note. That is the Grambling I knew, making people stand to their feet.

Being a part of The Epsilon Rho Chapter of Kappa Kappa Psi made you stay on your toes because the brothers held each other accountable when I marched in the band, and they helped me to become the man and Band Director I am today. I enjoyed my time in the World Famed because I learned life lessons, formed relationships with people from all over the world, which helped me mold my craft through the guidance of the directors. I would not change a thing because without my life experiences, I would not be who I am today. Being in the World Famed taught me a lot and my high school band program has blossomed from those lessons. In 2008 when I earned the A. "Andrew" Frank Martin Award for having the highest GPA in the fraternity that showed me that lofty standards have become the norm for me because I just want the best in life. This is what I love about HBCUs, they cultivate success.

While being a member of the World Famed, I also took care of business academically in all my other courses and finished to be eligible for graduation in Spring 2010. I always tell people it is never too late to finish because it is not how you start, it is how you finish and if I can do it, anyone can. Again, I would not change anything in my life because I have learned so much over the years. I am finishing my doctoral degree this summer so I can attest that the perseverance that I have learned from Grambling has prepared me to complete my doctoral journey. Long live thy Grambling State University World Famed Tiger Marching Band. HBCUs are the greatest.

# About Roderick Jefferson

Roderick Jefferson is the Director of Bands of the "The Huntington Band". He is currently in his 12th year at Huntington but previously he spent 8 years as the Assistant Band Director at Woodlawn High School. He has taken the band to LMEA Marching Festival, Large Ensemble Festivals and area Battle of The Bands winning no less than superior and majority 1st Place and Grand Champion. Under his reign: The Huntington Marching Band has performed in Washington D.C.'s National Independence Day Parade and the band has been invited to France, Italy, Czech Republic, Hawaii, New York, Chicago etc. The band has appeared in a nation tv show *Bayou Billionaires* on the CMT Network and was on the FOX commercial *The Passion* featuring Tyler Perry.

Mr. Jefferson began his teaching career at Woodlawn High School in Shreveport, LA. Mr. Jefferson is a native of Shreveport, Louisiana and attended Woodlawn High School. Upon graduation, he attended Grambling State University where he received a Bachelor's Degree in Instrumental Music Education. While at Grambling, he studied saxophone with Dr. Larry J. Pannell and conducting with Mr. Malcolm Spencer. He arranged for the World Famed Grambling State University Marching Band during the position of "Student Conductor" while in college and continues to till this day. Mr. Jefferson received his Master's Degree in 2013. He is currently working on his Doctoral Degree in Organizational Leadership at Grand Canyon University.

Mr. Jefferson is a member of: Louisiana Music Educators Association, National Association for Music Education, Kappa Kappa Psi National Honorary Band Fraternity, Red River United, Alpha Lambda Delta, and definitely not least Kappa Alpha Psi Fraternity.

# KAREN DERRICKSON

# OLD AGGIE SPIRIT

## Karen Derrickson

### North Carolina A&T State University

## No Excuses

Ahhhhhhhhh! The introduction to Cameo's song "Skin I'm In" was often played to energize the Blue and Gold Marching Machine (BGMM). This was heard outside of Frazier Hall on A&T's campus. Some stood on chairs, swaying while playing with the lights off and Doc or a Drum Major on the podium conducting. Dr. Johnny B. Hodge, Jr. was known as Doc. Tall and slender, he observed you through the bottom of his glasses when conversing. He was more than the director of bands; he was your father away from home. When you became a member, you met his expectations. You concentrated on your classes, learned new music and dance routines, attended sectionals, navigated adversities, and conducted yourself as a reputable A&T Aggie. Doc expected your best and tolerated no excuses!

## "In Storm and Sunshine"

Doc had no room for poor-quality instrumentalists. "Little girl, you need to practice!" Doc exclaimed, my first year. He continues with, "You are not where I require you to be. Yes, you are on third, but your position is still a vital piece of the band. You may not be number one in everything but know that you always bring something to the table." This position is like coming off the bench in sports. You have an important role, but the first trumpet is like a point guard, in my opinion. Our section was called Scream Machine. Some played such high notes that it sounded like a perfectly pitched scream. If you tried to scream, you better not hang over. Doc would surely point out how dreadful it sounded. When in the band room, or enclosed space, you may not catch the missed notes, but to the trained ear of Dr. Johnny B., he heard every single note, right and wrong.

Earsplitting wrong notes were heard when you watched the video on VHS. That's what "band heads" did in the 1990s. We were curious as to the playing style of other HBCU bands. Can they dance? Do they have 90s, which is lifting your knees so high that a 90-degree angle is formed? Most importantly, can they play? Sure, you can play songs you hear on the radio, but can you play a meticulous march, which illustrates more talent? Our march was "In Storm and Sunshine," composed by John C. Heed. There's a meticulous rhythmic pattern during the introduction that was problematic for many. Doc would point to you and say "play" individually. This would inform the band of your talent.

**"Up In the Morning, Before Day"**

Band camp consisted of shortened summers. You arrived at Frazier Hall days ahead of the fall semester. It resembled being an athlete. Dr. Kenneth Ruff, before being selected as A&T's Director of Bands, would scream, "To be early is to be on time. To be on time is to be late. To be late is to be ready for the next rehearsal." We'd hear this as we ran to practice at 4:57 am. Practice was from 5-7 am, 9-11 am, 1-3 pm, then 5-7 pm. As the semester began, practice was from 5-7 pm but over time, we realized it was 5 pm until Doc was satisfied.

Many days we attended sectionals, after rehearsal. My first Section Leader, Brian Millsap, never tolerated a sloppy trumpet player. He was a music major and meticulous, comparable to Doc. It didn't matter if you were first or third chair. All of this molded me into an integral piece of the BGMM.

"Gimme them bones" is what was yelled when Doc was ready to march to the practice field, the stadium for game day, or to return to the band room. Our trombones were the first few rows of instruments. We'd march through campus, practice on the field, then march back to Frazier Hall. The practice field is where the implementation of music and routine were integrated with your position on the field. Repetition is how we perfected our craft. "Take it to the hole" meant we were rehearsing the routine from start to finish. We'd be exhausted, hot, or cold, tired and wet from sweat or rain. To the hole, we went to perfect the upcoming show. This instilled a sense of pride in your presentation to the public and bled into my daily regime.

Returning to the band room was distinctive. Each section would showcase their high stepping or creative dancing skills. It seemed like it took hours for each section to march into the band room. Drummers played their unique cadences while sliding left to right and twirling their drumsticks. Some clashed cymbals between their legs while every section paraded inside. Last to enter were the auxiliary girls named Golden Delight, drum majors, and drummers, respectively.

## Small Band with A Big Sound

The band I wanted to challenge was Florida Agricultural and Mechanical University (FAMU). FAMU is huge, and they had a powerful sound. We finally traveled to FAMU. We alternated songs during breaks in the football game. The BGMM was considered "the small band with the big sound." We proved it when we played during the fifth quarter. The fifth quarter is the timeframe after a football game when HBCU bands would battle each other, displaying songs in their repertoire. The two university bands played a couple of songs as one combined band. It felt remarkable to be competitive yet respectful of the different styles of HBCU bands.

You heard the same songs often but different renderings. Which school had the best arrangement? Did it feature the song perfectly? Did they play with control, and was the song powerful? You would know by the chills you felt when the music resonated. Golden Delight was always astonishing. No one outclasses A&T's Golden Delight. They performed flawlessly to the songs in our repertoire.

Secretly, I practiced their routines in the mirror when I should have focused more on my trumpet.

**Aggies Everywhere**

Entering the Army was tough. It resembled activities learned in band camp from exercises, expectations, pride, leadership, and loyalty. Loyalty was on our BGMM gold t-shirts worn to the practice field. I was stationed in Germany from April 2001 to Dec 2007. Most who knew me in Germany affiliated me with A&T. They knew I was a proud Aggie alumna and marched in the BGMM. My Brigade Deputy Commander would often see me in the hallway and yell out, "Hey, Aggie! How's it going?" My response was, "Fine, Sir!" I smiled because he recognized my Aggie Spirit. When the movie *Drumline* arrived in theaters, Soldiers ran to tell me how much they loved the movie.

I ran into my Scream Machine brother, Anthony Lewis, while stationed in Germany. We gathered once a month unless one of us was deployed. We'd reminisce about the BGMM and discuss the Fifth Quarter, a band website created by an Aggie, Christy Walker.

Lessons learned in the BGMM prepared me for success throughout my military career. Doc's high expectations and Brian's attention to detail set me on the right path. I earned the rank of Staff sergeant within 5.5 years and later, the position of platoon sergeant. This position is habitually held by a higher-ranking Non-Commissioned Officer (NCO). I was the Runner-up for NCO of the Year for 5th Signal Command, and during the same year, my direct Soldier won Soldier of the Year.

While in Germany, I was selected by Dennis L. Via to be a commissioned officer. I led Soldiers into successful deployments during Operation Iraqi Freedom and Operation Enduring Freedom. I was ranked number one in my battalion, as a Lieutenant and again as a Captain. Recently, I was promoted, at my organization, to lead a team of network and cyber engineers.

## Grateful

I was naturally skilled at many activities, but entering a band with experts in comparison, challenged me. I learned not to give up, and if I want something, go get it. Playing third trumpet allowed me to understand my role in the organization. My part may not have been the one most wanted, but I played it with pride. From the lessons learned at A&T, I live a successful and accomplished life. My time in the BGMM was instrumental and I convey my Aggie Spirit, ubiquitously.

This is dedicated to my uncle, Gerald Derrickson, who grew up across from Frazier Hall. He loves the band. As a mentally challenged person, he would mimic the band with his plastic trumpet in hand as they marched to and from Frazier Hall. Band members would break ranks to shake hands or hug him. Gerald is in his 80s now but continues to smile when he thinks of the BGMM. Doc had a special place in his heart, because he allowed Gerald to interact when the band was in motion.

# About Karen Derrickson

United States (US) Army Major (retired) Karen C. Derrickson was born and raised in Greensboro, North Carolina. She graduated from James B. Dudley High School, where she was active in sports, additionally marching and concert bands. She attended North Carolina Agricultural and Technical State University (NC A&T SU) and played the trumpet in the Blue and Gold Marching Machine (BGMM) during her undergraduate studies.

Major (ret) Derrickson graduated with a Bachelor of Science degree in Graphic Communication Systems and Technological Studies in 1997 and a Master of Science degree in Technology Education in 1999, likewise from NC A&T SU.

Karen enlisted in the US Army in 2000 as a Multimedia Illustrator. Her dedication and professionalism, as a Staff Sergeant, marked her to be a Direct Select to Officer Candidate School, in 2007 by General (ret) Dennis L. Via. Major (ret) Derrickson was commissioned as a Signal Officer in 2008. She mastered radio and network communications and was selected to serve as a Functional Area Information Systems Engineering Officer in 2015. Major (ret) Derrickson completed her 20 years of honorable military service in July 2020 and continues to work in cybersecurity as a Department of Defense (DoD) Contractor. Her awards include the Bronze Star Medal, Meritorious Service Medals, Army Achievement Medals, North Atlantic Treaty Organization (NATO) Medal, Noncommissioned Officer Professional Development (NCOPD) Medals, Military Outstanding Volunteer Service Medal, and a few others. Karen was awarded the esteemed Bronze Order of Mercury and Order of Saint Barbara for high standards of integrity, service, competence, and contribution to the Signal Corps and Field Artillery, respectively.

Major (ret) Derrickson is a Doctor of Philosophy (PhD) candidate at Liberty University in Criminal Justice and Homeland Defense - Cybersecurity. She's a proud member of Tau Beta Sigma (TBS) National Honorary Band Sorority, Epsilon Pi Tau (EPT) International Honor Society for Technology, and Armed Forced Communications & Electronics Association (AFCEA) International.

# TRACIE MAY

# MENTORED TO GREATNESS

Tracie May

**Prairie View A&M University**

August 1993. I was excited and anxious to walk the campus of Prairie View A&M University. The weather was hot, and I was totally feeling free to be on my own. Walking to the band hall for the first time with my clarinet was a walk I'll never forget. My nerves were bad, and I feared the unexpected. I could only rely on my bubbly personality to get through what was to come. I had no idea who the band director was, and I only knew one person in the band at the time. I was the true definition of a crab. The only thing that kept replaying in my head was the movie School Daze and the hit sitcom, A Different World. Will PV be a version of the two combined? Will I survive the band camp for a band that was known for bringing the crowds to their feet? Will I have the confidence to follow in the shoes of those before me? The uncertainty was deafening and frightful, but I wanted to be there like a horn needed a musician. I was ready for the challenges I faced because I had to prove to my twin brother that I could do it. No, he did not doubt me. I simply had a strong urge to please him and make him proud of me. It was the first time we would not be together, and I needed the closeness of family while I was four hours away from home. As soon as I set foot into the aura of the band hall, I knew I was home, and I would be just fine, even as a crab.

The first few weeks were an eye opener for me. I had to learn to adjust in my lifestyle to be able to keep up with the demands of Prof Edwards. We practiced for hours upon hours. Keep in mind, Prairie View A&M University was in the middle of the longest losing streak in football history. That did not matter to any one of us. We were there because of the love of music and performance. It was that love for music, performance, crowd reaction and the feeling of accomplishment that kept me going. We would watch the football players walk to the field, practice, and then leave while we were still going back "to the hole." Prof Edwards made sure that everything was perfect before we left practice for the night. He would always tell us "I want your knees up to your lips!" Oh, and did he mean it. I remember dragging myself to my room on the 3rd floor of Banks Hall at 2:00 am thinking, "what have I gotten myself into?" Although those were my thoughts, I was not going to give up. I wanted this too bad not to "dig on in."

The night the crabs were being taught fast cadence, my knee was swollen and full of fluid. All I could think of was why me?? I stood on the sideline watching intensely as my clarinet section mastered the movements. Because I was on the sick and shut in list with my knee, I earned the crab name Crip. Many took my name to have a different meaning in the 90s because I always wore a blue bandana to tame my hair, but it was definitely because of the fluid on my knee that had me limping around for a short while. The next day, my determination would not allow me to stay on the sidelines. I got out there and mastered the fast cadence in one practice! I felt like I was unstoppable because others were working hard to master the skill while I was hanging with the upperclassmen. My bestie, Tiffany, was crab '91 and we were well on our way to making things happen in the clarinet section. That's when I decided to join Tau Beta Sigma National Honorary Band Sorority.

The year 1995 had arrived, I was 19 and living my best life. I named it the best and worst year of my life. Why? Because tragedy struck and changed the trajectory of my life forever. My twin, my brother, Travis, was murdered in the streets of my hometown, Ft. Worth, Texas. It was a case of being in the wrong place at the wrong time. It's true what they say about twins because I felt it. This was a huge blow for me, but I refused to let it take me out. The perseverance that I'd learned from Prof Edwards, Dr. Prof Phillips and Prof Jones kept me. I refused to stay at home because of the loss of my brother. I knew that I needed to remain in school to help take the pain away. I leaned on my sorority sisters of Tau Beta Sigma National Honorary Band Sorority, my fraternity brothers of Kappa Kappa Psi National Honorary Band Fraternity, my close friends, and the Marching Storm band. They showed me the true meaning of family, support, and taught me to never give up on myself no matter what the circumstances are. In doing so I was nominated as Miss Band in fall 1995. This was a major accomplishment for me! My band family held me in the highest esteem to represent them for the 1995-1996 academic year. I felt like I had arrived at the prestige that I was working towards for the Marching Storm Band.

Many have come before me and after me. Those before me helped to shape me into the marcher that I was. In the process, I found someone in my section to model and follow for my style of perfecting my marching and we called her Boo. She was the epitome of what Prof Edwards was looking for when it came to marching. I watched and watched and watched until I was able to mimic her moves perfectly. When it came time to come through Da Box (percussion section), I was beyond ready. I came through like a machine thanks to the influence of Boo. Tiffany and I would lead the clarinet section through Da Box and it was jumping from there on! My mentors were absolutely the truth!

Joining the Marching Storm Band under the expert tutelage of Professor George Edwards, Dr. Professor Mark Phillips and Professor Larry Jones was one of the best decisions I have ever made. The camaraderie, support and fellowship has been incomparable to anything I have experienced. The lessons of understanding that sleep is a luxury, "dig on in", "back in the hole" have been priceless. Because of the lessons learned on The Hill, I have accomplished goals that I NEVER thought I would accomplish. I have learned to teach children to follow their dreams no matter what their dreams are. Over the last 21 years I have learned to teach children to keep going regardless of your socioeconomic status, your family home life or your popularity. To seek the highest mountain to accomplish your dreams and God will take you to the end. When you have a solid support system, use it to the fullest. Family and friends will always be there to push you to be the best possible. No one wants to be the smartest or the best in their circle of friends. We always want to be around people who will help us to level up. Surround yourself with people that will take you to the next level. The Prairie View A&M University Marching Storm Band certainly did it for me. Find someone or something who will certainly do it for you. You can expect nothing but greatness as the outcome.

I'm forever grateful and in debt to the Marching Storm Band. Peace from the Purple and Gold!

Crab '93 ~ Crip
Tau Beta Sigma
Fall '94
#1 lb. Puppy
Improvisation

# About Tracie May

Tracie May is currently in her 21st year of working in education. She has worked with elementary, middle, and high school students throughout Houston, Texas and Fort Worth, Texas. She started out as a College & Career Readiness Coach by assisting high school students to gain admission into the college of their choice. This also included applying for scholarships, financial aid, and numerous college tours throughout the United States. The love and passion she has for assisting students in meeting their goals is incomparable.

Tracie began her educational career at the tender age of 2 years old while attending Temple Christian Private School with her twin brother, Travis. While there, her love for music grew as she was introduced to the likes of the 70's era of rhythm and blues by her parents. Growing up with her father, who played saxophone in the Presidential parade when John F. Kennedy was assassinated in Dallas, Texas, Tracie took a liking to instruments. It was in 2nd grade when she was introduced to the Recorder. She later learned to play the violin alongside her twin for 2 years. Wanting to be just like her big sister, Jackie, she followed in her sisters' footsteps and learned to play the clarinet. I know you are wondering, what did mom do? She was our family athlete and not the musician.

She is a proud product of Fort Worth Independent School District. While matriculating, her guidance from her family of educators encouraged her to dream big and follow her dreams. She attended the Stop Six Pyramid of schools for the majority of education and graduated from Paul Laurence Dunbar High School. Throughout her time, she attended the Magnet Program at Dunbar Middle School, matriculated to O.D. Wyatt International Baccalaureate Program, and completed her studies in the Advanced Honors Program at P.L. Dunbar High School. She went on to attend Prairie View A&M

University where she earned her Bachelor of Science in Health and a Master in Human Sciences with an emphasis in Marriage & Family Therapy.  She later attended Tarleton State University where she was accepted into the Educational Leadership doctoral program. She hopes to complete the program.

MORGAN

# The Magnificent Marching Baloo

**Marcus Neal**

**Morgan State University**

Let's journey back to the late 90s. Here it is, the spring of 1997 and I'm trying to figure out "where should I attend college?" On one hand I considered UMBC because I was a part of the upward bound program during the summer of 94… but it didn't feel right for me. The brochure for North Carolina A&T looked nice and my family is from Greensboro. I thought to myself, "Maybe I should be an Aggie… nah that's too far." Oh yeah, that nice Band director from Morgan State just came to my high school band banquet, maybe I should go there. Their mascot is the Bears, my nickname is Baloo and he's a Bear, it's here in Baltimore. I think I'm going to Morgan State!

So now here I am, a freshman trombone player in the Magnificent Marching Machine. Since I wasn't exposed to much HBCU band culture in high school besides a few band tapes of Howard thanks to an Edmondson Alum who marched there, everything was new to me. The one thing I loved the best though was learning fanfares as a section. Fanfares are short songs performed only by your section and not the whole band. Sometimes they're called "Punches" or "Riffs" based on what region you're from. I remember the first one my section leader Jarrett Miles (one of Dr. Melvin Miles' twin sons in the band) taught us, was Pony by Ginuwine. When we stood up for the first time to play it, I was nervous but as we played, I saw how the crowd loved it and I was hooked! He would go on to teach us a few more for the upcoming battles but I had a great idea for one! I told him we needed to play the old HBO Movie intro as a fanfare. He liked that idea, arranged it and taught it just before our trip to California for the Gold Coast Classic.

Now it's time to take the show on the road.  We flew cross country for this big classic in San Diego against Howard's Showtime Marching band.  The night before the game Jarrett taught     us a new fanfare and he titled it "Wimbledon" like the Tennis Grand Slam.  Since it's only six of us, he tells me it's my job to hold down the bass line with my freshmen sisters Kesha and Chevonne.  Game day comes and we finally get to face another section, Howard's "T-Bone Express."  It's like eighteen of them and only six of us, but that didn't mean anything to us, we're the LEGION OF BONES!  So after a good battle between the two of us I felt really good about what other sections we may face.  Little did I know we were about to have our hands full the next week in Hampton, Virginia.

Their name is "Slide-Force" and as my good friend and frat brother Prunejuice would say "And don't forget the hyphen!" Man… . These were some playing cats! They were playing fanfares against us that were arranged really well, and they had some range too!  The main fanfares that stuck out was Tri-Star Movie intro, the theme song from the 70s sitcom "What's Happening" and the theme song from "Super Mario Bros."  I'm man enough to admit, they got us that cold day in November, but little did they know they sparked a new thrill for your boy Baloo!  I had no idea fanfares could be so creative and out of the box like that.

Now it's my sophomore year.  The section is now run by "Fearless Leader" Lionel Lyles and it's time for me to step up as a leader among the section.  Lionel and I were both on the same page about writing newer, more creative material.  I told him about how I was talking with my best friend Twone about how Slide-Force plays Mario Bros. theme.  Twone suggested we should play "The Legend of Zelda" theme back at them.  Lionel's eyes lit up and he jumped right on it.  Keep in mind this is 1998, we're on the verge of the digital world so most of our music is still handwritten.  It took Lionel a few days but he did it!  I couldn't wait until we saw Slide-Force again to premiere it!  So once again, the last game of the year, in cold

November, this time Hampton makes the trip to Baltimore and we're ready!  Third Quarter hits, and now it's our time to shine!  They play their stuff and we wait until they play Super Mario Bros., and we hit 'em with Zelda!  Our band went nuts because they didn't expect anything like that.  I could tell from the other side of the field they weren't expecting it either.  I was so glad I had my good friend Chris in the stands recording this.  This was before YouTube so if you wanted to see it, you had to have someone record it and put it on a "Band Tape."  From that day, both sections have had a mutual respect for one another.

Now we're crossing over into the digital world of HBCU Band Culture, and it just so happened Christy and Mike started the 5th Quarter on January 19, 1999.  I quickly made friends with band members from other HBCUs.  There were so many other HBCU Bands I never heard of from my lack of exposure from growing up in Baltimore.  Yeah, I heard of the Bayou Classic, but only knew of the football game, I never watched the halftime show.  This is how I learned about The Marching 100, The Human Jukebox, The Blue & Gold Marching Machine, The Aristocrats of Bands, and many more.  We began to trade tapes with one another so we could see what each other's programs had to offer.  Not only that, but now I have begun to see how competitive it was amongst our HBCU Bands.  One poster in particular was a member of Slide-Force and his username was "Scream Bone X".  Now you may know him as Dr. Thomas L. Jones, Jr current director of bands at Hampton University.  Thomas would always talk about how high he and other members of his section could play.  That sounded like a challenge to me, so we used that as motivation to learn to scream on trombone as well.

Over the course of the next few years while marching at Morgan, LOB would devise a game plan for every section we were going to face.  We knew some sections were about playing with power, some about playing smooth, and some even making their fanfares personal.  One year I drove a red pick-up truck that was identical to Dr. Miles'.

One night a bunch of members from Morgan and Howard's band got together to hang out in Baltimore.  My truck broke down on the highway and members of Howard's band dubbed it Fred Sanford's truck.  That fall, Sparkle Mitchell made sure her trombone section T-Bone Express played the Fred Sanford Theme against us.  We were dying in the stands.  Sparkle just so happened to have a girl group that performed on the Apollo Amateur night.  We learned the same song they were booed for and debated if we should play it back next year.

Speaking of Apollo, Norfolk's trombone section "Horny Horns" faced a similar fate on Amateur night, and we considered mocking them as well.  Instead, we decided to learn their band's signature song "Behold."  During their homecoming of 2002 we were battling them, and they wouldn't play back.  After about two songs with no response, a guy in my section named Joey said "Baloo… you know what we have to do."  We knew we'd get in trouble, but we didn't care.  We called it off and played it perfectly, even Maurice hit the high note clean, and he had been missing it all week.  The look of all those shiny helmets jumping up and down in rage was well worth Renard telling us to sit down.  We just knew it may be rough getting back to the buses after that one.  The Spartans were mad at us on the 5th Quarter that week talking about how we could get sued because the song is copyrighted. "Wasn't nobody making money off of a fanfare!" We laughed in sectionals all week reading those comments. To this day, I would pay good money to someone who has this on tape.

## About Marcus Neal

A native of Baltimore, Maryland, Marcus began his musical journey at West Baltimore Middle School under the guidance of Bettye T McLeod. He would go on to learn Baritone and Trombone. It was his freshmen year at Edmondson-Westside High School where he would receive his more affectionately known nickname "Baloo". While attending The National Treasure Morgan State University, Marcus participated in various ensembles including Jazz Band, Symphonic Band, and the Magnificent Marching Machine. A dual graduate of Morgan State having received his bachelor's degree in music in 2011 and a Master of Arts degree in Teaching in 2015.

His collegiate accolades include section leader of the trombone section, the Legion of Bones, and a charter member of Phi Mu Alpha Sinfonia Fraternity, Pi Eta Chapter. His other affiliations include member of the Baltimore Ravens Marching Band, St. John's Lodge #5 M.W. Prince Hall Grand Lodge MD, and Baltimore Area Alumni Association of Phi Mu Alpha Sinfonia chartering member. Marcus has been teaching in Baltimore City Public Schools since 2011 having served several schools throughout the district and as assistant director of bands at his alma mater Edmondson for nine years. Marcus is happily married to his wife Bridgette, who he met while marching together at Morgan. They have three wonderful children, Melanie, Morgan and Alexander.

# SONJA DAVIS AND CALVIN DAVIS

# Married to the Machine
## Sonja Davis and Calvin Davis
## North Carolina A&T State University

## Golden Reflections

It was the mid-80s and I was a 7th grader already with a dream. It was a cool fall afternoon and I had just experienced the most amazing University Day at North Carolina A&T. WOW…. the band, the cheerleaders, and the atmosphere. It was a total vibe. It was at that moment that I knew I was going to be a Future Aggie.

Back home, in Charlotte, NC, I had been dancing since the age of two with the BC Brown Sugar Dance Group and later with Miss Donna's School of Dancing and was a competitive dancer by 6th grade. I was also a Pop-Warner and Jr. High cheerleader. I started playing the clarinet in 5th grade and continued at Myers Park High School. With my many talents, I just knew I was meant to use them at A&T.

Fast forward to the first day of band camp during my Junior year in Myers Park's Marching band. My band director asked if any females were interested in auditioning for color guard. I figured since I was a dancer, it would be a wonderful opportunity to try something new; learn how to twirl flags and get a chance to dance. I excelled in color guard that year, but unforeseen circumstances wouldn't allow me to continue my Senior year. However, I continued playing my clarinet in the symphonic band and because of my musical abilities, I was offered a band scholarship at NC A&T by former band director, Dr. Johnny B. Hodge.

On the first day of band camp, I remember being excited and scared all at the same time. I didn't fully know what to expect but I knew it would be different from my high school Corp style days.

Well, just like high school, Dr. Hodge had a meeting with the freshman girls and offered us a chance to audition for Golden Delight Auxiliary where they twirled flags and danced, and I was like, "Sign Me Up!" The blessing was that I was still on a band scholarship as a member of Golden Delight during the Fall, while still being in band year-round, playing my clarinet in the Symphonic Band. Also due to my abilities during my Junior and Senior year, Dr. Hodge made me learn how to play the Alto and Bass Clarinet for our Spring Concerts.

Some major highlights being a part of the BGMM are marching across campus on Fridays in my majorette boots, the Aggie/Eagle Classics, and our 1993 Homecoming against Howard University being televised on BET. Others include In 1994, pledging Tau Beta Sigma National Honorary Band Sorority, being a Golden Delight captain with my best friend, facing off with Southern University at the Circle City Classic and meeting my future husband, Calvin Davis (BGMM trumpet player) in the band, although we didn't start dating until Spring 1996. SN: I always said long before we started dating, he was checking me out in my gold sequin uniform…lol!

So many great times and memories from being a part of such an amazing organization. My family and I go to Homecomings (now known as GHOE – the Greatest Homecoming on Earth) and Calvin and I are preparing our daughter and son to be a part of the next generation of amazing Aggies!

**Memories of the Culture**

My love for North Carolina A&T State University began when I had an older cousin to graduate with his engineering degree. This love grew after I visited the campus in 1990 when my math and science academic program held its annual day festivities there. This annual day just so happened to fall on the same day as "Aggie Fest" (before it was scaled back IYKYK). Everywhere you looked, there was black culture that just made me feel at home.

My marching band origin started with West Charlotte High School in Charlotte, NC. I had been playing trumpet since the 5th grade and was very comfortable in a show style marching band. Knowing that I had been accepted and planning to attend North Carolina A&T State University to major in mechanical engineering, a full year in advance, I had plenty of time to study HBCU marching bands. During football season, I would park the TV on the BET channel every Saturday afternoon waiting to see if a black college football game would be televised. Watching those halftime shows only fueled my anticipation of joining the Blue and Gold Marching Machine. After observing several halftime shows over time, I started noticing subtle differences and similarities from band to band; the marching styles, musical styles, drilling styles and the seriousness of them all. Not one time did I see a band member grin or crack a smile. It didn't take long to figure out that HBCU band culture is all business and about school pride.

When I arrived at my first BGMM band camp in August 1994, I could barely contain my excitement. Before the trumpet section was issued instruments, we were told that we would be playing on brand new Holton 'bent' trumpets and that we needed to take good care of them. After I get my horn and put the mouthpiece in, I'm ready to start blowing! Unfortunately, the great Dr. Johnny B. Hodge put the brakes on that REAL quick. Doc told us to pull out the sheet music to the "In Storm and Sunshine" march and it didn't take long to find out why either. He went around the entire band room and asked each person to play the first several measures by themselves. Whether you played it well or messed up, it seemed like he could relate your playing to where you were from. Thank goodness I was a pretty decent trumpet player because Doc did not mind embarrassing you one bit.

Our first outside practice as a band started at 5am sharp! The purpose of early practices was to learn marching style basics like whistle blow-off, long halt, horn swing, knee lift, drum major commands, and the movements to go along. We also learned basic squad maneuvers like slants, pinwheels, and 'turn-to-the-rear.' The band had to master these basics in order to begin learning the first field show later that day. The 2nd practice would be for the field show that went from 9-11am where we would be put into our squads of 4 members and learn the maneuvers and counts for the first game's halftime show. After that practice concluded, it was a mad dash to the cafeteria for lunch. There would be a 3rd practice that went from 1-3pm which would solely focus on music. Finally, the 4th practice was a combination of music and field show rehearsal that required the band to march across campus to the practice field in parade formation. In my freshman year, the first parade song we learned was, "Don't Stop Till You Get Enough" by Michael Jackson. We played that song so much marching across campus that I still remember how to play it after 29 years!

My first game as a member of the NC A&T Blue and Gold Marching Machine couldn't have been any more memorable. We started the season off against our biggest rival, North Carolina Central University in the Aggie-Eagle Eagle Classic. The game was held at NC State's Carter-Finley Stadium which at the time had a capacity of nearly 50,000 fans. I still remember that it rained earlier that day and was worried that the weather would keep some fans away. Marching into the stadium, I could hear the Aggie fans cheer over the drum cadence as the band came into view. All of the music rehearsals, 5am practices, standing at attention in 90 plus degree heat with sweat and gnats in your face, culminated into my first halftime as part of the BGMM. As Doc would say, "IT'S ON!!" Our downfield that game was an arrangement of Parliament's "One Nation Under a Groove" into a short version of "Knee Deep." That was followed by a tribute to Africa where the band executed the formation of the continent. After that, it was into concert formation where we cranked up on Janet Jackson's "Anytime, Anyplace," which would become one of our staple songs from that season.

One of the many highlights of my first year in the band was traveling to Indianapolis, Indiana to play Southern University at the annual Circle City Classic. Back then, this game was a big deal and often brought two schools who wouldn't normally meet during a typical football season. The game was held at the RCA Dome, home of the Indianapolis Colts NFL team. This was an anticipated game because Southern's band was televised every year in the Bayou Classic and was known to have a very good band. This game included both bands to perform two field shows. One during halftime and a post-game Battle of the Bands show. We knew we had an 'average' show for halftime but weren't holding back anything for the post-game show. Our post game show was longer than our typical halftime show. It was our first show plus an extended "Golden Delight" dance feature to Aretha Franklin's "Deeper Love." The show concluded with a dance routine that received a loud ovation from the nearly 60,000 fans. Southern's show was very underwhelming and looked unorganized. There was no question who won that battle. ;-)

## About Sonja Davis and Calvin Davis

Calvin J. Davis was born and raised in Charlotte, NC to his loving parents Charles and Alphia Davis. After graduating from West Charlotte High School, he attended North Carolina A&T State University to major in mechanical engineering. After earning his undergraduate degree in 1999, he was offered a job in St. Louis, MO working for electrical manufacturer Square D Company as a technical sales specialist. After a two-and-a-half-year stint Calvin moved on to Engineered Air Systems Inc. (later named DRS Technologies) as a design engineer. Initially unbeknownst to him, it was later discovered that Calvin was the first black engineer hired by the company which had been established in 1942. At DRS, he worked on various projects as a defense contractor for all branches of the military including the replacement of the environmental control system for the Minuteman III intercontinental ballistic missile. Eventually, Calvin made his way back to the electrical distribution industry as a Customer Support Specialist for ABB Group.

Outside of work, Calvin serves as deacon at his church and volunteers with the youth ministry. In his spare time, Calvin enjoys cooking on the grill, listening to jazz music, and spending time with family.

He has been married to his lovely wife, Sonja Davis of 22 years and they are parents to their daughter, Courtney and son, Calvin Jr.

---

Sonja Willingham Davis was born and raised in Charlotte, NC. She is the daughter of David and Ola Willingham III. After graduating from Myers Park High School in 1992, she entered North Carolina A&T State University as a business major. After earning a

Bachelor of Science Degree in Business Administration and a Bachelor of Science Degree in Office Administration, she went on to obtain her Master of Business Administration in 2000 from Pfeiffer University at Charlotte. For over 20 years Sonja has worked in Corporate America in various industries from Public Service, Healthcare, Janitorial and Real Estate. In 2022, she became an educator at Charlotte Mecklenburg School as an Elementary Dance Teacher at a Creative Arts School. In the Fall of 2023, she will become a middle school CTE Business Education Teacher, teaching Beginner Keyboarding and Entrepreneur. She also is the Lead Recreational Dance Teacher at Miss Donna's School of Dancing Sardis location teaching tap, jazz, ballet, lyrical and hip hop.

Sonja is a proud member of Tau Beta Sigma National Honorary Band Sorority, having pledged in the Theta Zeta Chapter at NC A&T in 1994 and Delta Sigma Theta Sorority Incorporated in 2004 with the St. Louis Metropolitan Alumnae Chapter. She is also a member of St. Paul Baptist Church where she serves as the Director of the Liturgical Dance Ministry and as a volunteer for Children's Church.

In her spare time, Sonja enjoys dancing, traveling, watching HGTV, listening to jazz music, and spending time with family.

She currently resides in Matthews, NC with her college sweetheart & husband, Calvin J. Davis, of 22 years. They are the proud parents of daughter Courtney and son Calvin Jr., both whom they are grooming to be Future Aggies!

# LANITRA DEAN

# Entertainment Tonight
## LaNitra Dean
### Prairie View A&M University

I can never forget the blistering heat on move-in day to start my HBCU journey as a college student at Prairie View A&M University. I, with the assistance of my family, was loading the family truck with all of the items that I would need for my dorm room. It was a Saturday, August 10, 2002, and I was hours away from embarking on an experience of a lifetime. There were so many thoughts in my mind as I loaded the bed of the truck. Will this be like high school? Will this be worse? Will I get to know everyone? What do I need to expect? As I am getting this done, I receive a call from my close friend and soon to be college roommate Grace Dada. My parents would be helping her get situated on campus as well. Due to reasons that I can no longer remember, we arrived so late to the campus that we were unable to check into the dorm. We had to immediately report to Hobart Taylor Thomas also known as the band hall. When we arrived, we were met by oldheads. They let us know that we would be with them until we could check into our dorm the next day. I must admit I was a bit intimidated by them. I was 5'8" and 120 lbs soak and wet. In any case, the women welcomed us with open arms and allowed us to stay the night at their off-campus residence. The next day Grace and I woke up bright and early to check into our dorm. We were unable to set things up because we had to report to band camp after receiving our keys. The heat during band camp is a special kind of hell. I am unsure if it's the same heat now 21 years later. During band camp and all of our crab year, freshmen had to wear a white t-shirt to signify someone new to the band program. It wasn't any different from my high school experience. Even though I didn't go to the Army after high school, I still felt like I was in the military going through bootcamp. There were early mornings of running around campus and exercising, eating breakfast and then learning music. Any time we were in the band hall, on the field, or in practice sessions we were to be locked up. Meaning, we were not supposed to move a MUSCLE or speak unless spoken to! We were silenced but only to learn the ins and outs of the organization. I can honestly say that you learn so much more when you can only listen and observe. Discipline was one of many focuses during band camp. Discipline and focus was driven into crabs as soon as they touched down onto Prairie View's campus. I can attest to this day that discipline and focus is still a part of my everyday life.

During band camp we were introduced to Professor George Edwards, Professor William McQueen and Professor Larry Jones. Professor George Edwards, also known as Prof Ed, was the head band director. He was a man not very tall in stature, with a bald head, but you could see passion for music coursing through his veins and burning in his eyes. Prof Ed was an extraordinary person. He carried himself as though he was the father of every band student under his direction. You could always see his love for the Marching Storm band as he walked through ranks and the band hall with so much intensity and fire for the program that he was instrumental in building. Prof McQueen and Prof Jones were like the uncles of the band. You know the uncles at the cookout with the sandals and socks hanging out by the pit? Well, that was those two men. Their presence was fatherly but also along the lines of favored uncles. These three men shaped my life in many ways through their leadership and dedication to their band students.

After my freshman year, I became involved with the dance committee. The dance committee is a group of handpicked individuals by the drum majors for their dancing ability, ability to create choreography, and for their ability to teach the choreography. My sophomore year, Larry Allen, a drum major at the time, selected me to be a part of the dance committee. I was excited to use my gift of creative movement to assist with the creation of the band dance for halftime. I went to work reviewing music videos from BET and MTV for choreography ideas as well as creating choreography of my own. I assisted with the dance committee from 2003-2008. One year me and Gloria Lott, decided to use choreography from Michael Jackson's "Remember the Time" video. We took hours learning the choreography and perfecting it. If we didn't perfect the moves then the choreography would get cut. Well, we eventually got it polished and taught it to the band. I was instrumental in many of the most iconic halftime dance routines of that time. While working on the dance committee for the band and performing during the halftime shows, I decided that it wasn't enough. I craved dance so much that when I wasn't dancing to music, I missed it. It was like losing a part of myself. The music played was beautiful and lively but the movement of my body was non-existent at times. I decided to form my own hip hop dance group on PV's campus and named it The Get Fresh Crew. The Get Fresh Crew and all its members became well known and recognized for participation in talent shows and other performances on campus. The Get Fresh Crew introduced me to a plethora of opportunities on the Hill. One opportunity that I really enjoyed was the chance to choreograph fraternity pageants. My first pageant that I choreographed was the Ms. Krimson and Kream pageant for Kappa Alpha Psi. I was approached by my crab brother Jason Hooey, who was a member of the fraternity. After choreographing that pageant, I was selected by Gary Hill of Phi Beta Sigma to choreograph the Lady of the Dove pageant. I provided choreography for the LOTD pageant two consecutive years. I can honestly look back and say without a show of a doubt that my involvement with the Marching Storm, my love for music, and my ability to dance opened up these opportunities for me.

My participation with PVAMU's Marching Storm provided me with so many jewels for living life, friends for networking, chances to apply the use of silence when needed, as well taught me discipline and focus. As of today, I use all of these strengths passed on to me through my time at PVAMU to further my career and my passions. I learned from the band that "Sleep is a luxury". I learned that in order to climb up the ladder of success, I need to put in the work. I learned sacrifice, determination, and how to remain resilient while facing adversity. I am proud of my choice in selecting PVAMU as my HBCU of choice as well as my participation in the Marching Storm program. I truly believe within my heart and soul that I was a member of "The Best Band in the Land". I am thankful to Prairie View for producing a productive panther. Without PVAMU and the Marching Storm I wouldn't be where I am today.

# About LaNitra Dean

LaNitra LaChic Dean, was born in Houston, TX, to parents Edsel B. Dean Jr. and Gladys Dean (nee Ausbie). She is the only girl and middle sister of deceased brothers Patrick Ausbie (August 2021) and Gabriel Dean (April 2020). Her love of music and performing started early due to her parent's musical taste. On Friday and Saturday evenings in the early 1990s, her nights with the family were spent listening to blues, soul, funk, and R&B. As a natural performer, LaNitra's parents would have her entertain family and friends by singing hits from the 60s-80s and performing the latest dance moves of the 90s. Her mother and father also listened to jazz, rock, and pop music.

When Ms. Dean was eight years old, her older brother Patrick, who was a singer, decided to join his middle school band. Patrick chose to play the saxophone. Her parents bought their son Patrick the saxophone but also bought a clarinet as well. After school, Patrick taught his little sister everything that he learned about reading music. He even had other clarinet players teach him things about the clarinet so that he could share it with her. Even though she had dreams of becoming a dancer, she started to show an interest in music.

In 1995, her family moved from the Kashmere Gardens area of Houston to the Lakewood neighborhood which changed her school district from Houston ISD to North Forest ISD. LaNitra enrolled into R. E. Kirby Middle School and decided to begin her band journey. She was under the direction of Mr. Roderick Kennedy (PVAMU and Marching Storm Alumni) and Mr. William "Bill" Singletary. These men helped to further cultivate her musical passions. During her middle school years, she was section leader of the clarinet section, learned to play saxophone, received numerous awards for UIL Solo and Ensemble performances, and was allowed to use her love for dance during the football game halftime routines.  She was first introduced to PVAMU's Marching Storm band through the yearly event the Band Extravaganza.  This event showcased all of the bands in the North Forest school district as well as exposed band students and audiences to university bands such as PVAMU and TSU.  After performing in her first Band Extravaganza and watching the university marching bands perform, LaNitra had an idea of how far she could go with her musical interests.

In 1998, LaNitra enrolled in M.B. Smiley High School and began performing with the Marching Quake band. The Marching Quake band was under the direction of Mr. Gerald Stewart and Mr. Mark Gordon (PVAMU and Marching Storm Alumni). The Marching Quake band was modeled after the Marching Storm band of PVAMU. While in the band, LaNitra began using her love for dance more by assisting with the choreography for the band's dance routines for halftime shows. This not only allowed her to further connect with music but it also gave her the opportunity to express herself through movement, use her creativity, and teach the choreography to the band.  Black high school bands in the 90s and early 2000s derived their high energy halftime performances from HBCU bands. LaNitra continued to excel in band and as a musician. She was again awarded for multiple UIL Solo and Ensemble competitions. She learned to play bass clarinet and alto clarinet for the symphonic band. In her senior year, she was the section leader of the clarinet section and an integral part of the leadership within the band. In her senior year she had a difficult choice to make. Would she enroll in college or go to the military? LaNitra decided to go to the military. She took the ASVAB test, completed paperwork with an Army recruiter, and had a ship out date. However, in January 2002 her father informed her that he would not prefer for her to go to the Army. After that conversation, she immediately began applying to colleges. She settled on the one school that she knew felt like home, Prairie View A&M University. This began her HBCU journey which you will soon read about.

Now, she is a mother of one daughter, Jenesis Edmond and a caregiver to her father. LaNitra works in the energy sector full time analyzing and researching customer service data to improve customer service relations. In her spare time, she loves to travel and see the world with her daughter and spend time in nature. They have visited the pyramids of Giza in Egypt, ancient structures in Greece, and the serene islands of the Philippines. Today, she is still using her passion for music and dance. She works part time as a Group Fitness Instructor for multiple gyms in the Houston area. She choreographs routines for Zumba, cycling, and HIIT fitness classes to a wide variety of music. Her daughter is following in her musical footsteps as a flutist. Maybe one day you all will read of her HBCU band journey as well.

**AD Bonner Music**

CEO/Founder: Adrain Bonner

📱 817-300-3995

✉ adbonnermusic@gmail.com

**AG Management & Business Consulting**

CEO/Founder: Gabriel Langley

🌐 www.agmbc.com

**Alexander G. Events**

CEO/Founder: Nathan Alexander Kemp

📱 Nathan A. Kemp, 336-706-1422

📱 Brooke G. Kemp, 336-944-4768

✉ alexgevents20@gmail.com

**All Seasoning 20**

CEO/Founder: Hepston H. Henry II

📷 @allseasoning20

👍 @allseasoning20

🐦 @allseasoning20

♪ @allseasoning20

📱 336-265-1277

✉ allseasoning20@gmail.com

🌐 www.allseasoning20.com

**Allen Financial Solutions**

CEO/Founder: Jay Allen

📷 @jay83allen

👍 @Jay Allen

✉ allen.jonathan83@gmail.com

**The Alli Group, LLC**
**Real Estate Management**
Founders: Lawrence & Nickia Alli
@thealligroupllc
nickia.alli@gmail.com
www.thealligroupllc.com

**April Shell Consulting, LLC**
**Living Stress Free**
CEO/Founder: April Shell
@aprilnshell
@aprilnshell
@anshelltweets
@aprilshell
aprilnshell@gmail.com

**AMMEA**
President: Ernest Stackhouse
ej.stackhouse@gmail.com
www.ammea.org

**Ashley Little Enterprises, LLC**
CEO/Founder: Dr. Ashley Little
@_ashleyalittle
@Ashley Little
aalittle08@gmail.com
www.ashleylittleenterprises.com

**The Ancestor Key**
CEO/Founder: Ja'el Gordon
504-356-1466
theancestor@gmail.com

**The Self-care Doc**

CEO/Founder:

Dr. Raushannah Johnson-Verwayne
*Licensed Clinical Psychologist &
Wellness Coach*

@ @Ask Dr RJ

f @Ask Dr RJ

www www.AskDrRJ.com

**Assurance Tax & Accounting
Group, LLC**

CEO/Founder:

Kimberlee Collins-Walker
8676 Goodwood Blvd., Ste. 102
Baton Rouge, LA 70876

225-757-7518

kim@assurancetaxbr.com

www www.assurancetaxbr.com

**Baker & Baker Realty, LLC**

CEO/Founder: Christopher Baker

@ @seedougieblake

f @Christopher D. Baker

baker.christopher@gmail.com

**Balance Candle Bar**

CEO/Founder: Lacey B. Evans

www www.shopbalanceco.com

# B G B

### B a l d   G u y s   B a k e

**Bald Guys Bake, LLC**

CEO/Founder: Torey Searcy

info@baldguysbake.com

www www.baldguysbake.com

**Beautiful Body & More, LLC**

CEO/Founder: Melody Scott

318-716-1507
318-716-1508 fax

@ @Beautifulbodyandmore

f @Beautiful Body & More, LLC

www www.beautifulbodyandmore.com

**The Black Techies/Podcast**

CEO/Founder: Herbert L. Seward, III

*Where black culture meets the world of technology.*

www www.theblacktechies.com

**BLKWOMENHUSTLE**

CEO/Founder: Lashawn Dreher

@blkwomenhustle

@Blk Women Hustle

info@blkwomenhustle.com

**Block Band Music & Publishing, LLC**

CEO/Founder: D. Rashad Watters

919-698-2560

blockbandmusic@gmail.com

**Blue Street Pools**

CEO/Founder: Mark Jones

504-502-7655

bluestreetpools@gmail.com

**Boardroom Brand, LLC**

CEO/Founder: Samuel Brown, III

@_gxxdy

samuel.brown.three@gmail.com

**Body to Sole**

CEO/Founder: Megan Daniels

225-877-8597

bodytosolefitness@gmail.com

**Booked Cafe Books**

CEO/Founder: Kierra Jones

@Booked Cafe Books

@Booked Cafe Books

contact@bookedcafebooks.com

www.bookedcafebooks.com

**Brooks Art Collective**

CEO/Founder: LaToya Brooks

@brooksartcollective

@brooksartcollective

brooksartcollective@gmail.com

**Bound By Conscious Concepts**

CEO/Founder: Kathryn Lomax

@msklovibes223

@Klo-Kathryn Lomax

972-638-9823

klomax@bbconcepts.com

**BZAR STUDIOZ**

CEO/Founder: Steven Baltazar

bzarstudioz@gmail.com

www.bzarstudioz.com

**Braveheart Medical Mission**

CEO/Founder: Erica Rogers

erogers9483@gmail.com

## Caleb T. Dunbar Photography

CEO/Founder: Caleb T. Dunbar

@calebtdunbarphotography

@Caleb T. Dunbar Photography

318-403-4593

calebtdunbar@gmail.com

www.calebtdunbar.com

## Cici's Freelance Services

CEO/Founder:
Courtney "Cici" Walker, MPA

@cicisfreelanceservices

225-288-8216

cicisfreelanceservices@gmail.com

## Campaign Engineers

CEO/Founder: Chris Smith

@csmithatl

csmithl911@gmail.com

## Cjenk The Agency: Creative Concierge, LLC

CEO/Founder: Chasmin Jenkins

chasminjenkins@gmail.com

## Chef Batts

CEO/Founder: Keith Batts

@chefbatts

booking@chefbatts.com

## Color Wheel Therapy

CEO/Founder: Kiandra Daniels

469-251-2418

kiandra.daniels@colorwheeltherapy.com

www.colorwheeltherapy.com

**Commit 2 Life Fitness**

CEO/Founder: Joseph T. Shaw III

@commit2lifefitness

**The Bitter Suite Podcast**

*Apple & Spotify*

@thebittersuite2020

www.commit2life.com

**CreativeED Consulting, LLC**

CEO/Founder: Dr. William J. Earvin

wjeconsulting@icloud.com

**Cultural Resources**

CEO/Founder:

Corey "Mr. Hanky" Dennard

@culturalresources

amrhankybeat@gmail.com

**Curves & Gains**

CEO/Founder: Patrice Murphy

@curvesandgaines

curvesandgains@gmail.com

www.curvesandgains.com

**Da Edge 1 Productions**

CEO/Founder: Garrett Edgerson

@daedge1pro

www.daedge1pro.com

**Daily Life Managements LLC**

CEO/Founder:

Kristy Lashaun Burrell

504-390-9949

**Dapper Dillon**

CEO/Founder: Shaquille Dillon

✉ shaquille.dillon@gmail.com

**Dee Ree Hair Co**

CEO/Founder: Desiree R. Dawson

✉ desireeshanecedawson@yahoo.com

**DD Jones Enterprise**

CEO/Founder: Darcele Jones-Horton

✉ darceleh@bellsouth.net

**Deroune Services, LLC**

CEO/Founder: Marina Zeno

☎ 337-418-0785

**DDL Entertainment**

CEO/Founder: Darryl Lassister

✉ darryldlassiter@msn.com

**Dorian Troy Studios**

CEO/Founder: Dorian Davis

✉ dorian@doriantroystudios.com

**Dr. Ashanti Says, LLC**
CEO/Founder: Dr. Ashantia Says
www www.drashantisays.com
www https://linktr.ee/drashantisays

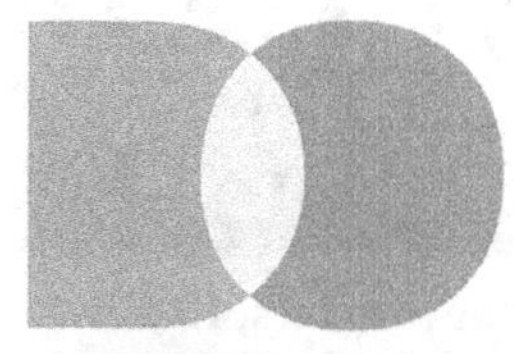

**Dream.Org**
CEO/Founder: Kasheef Wyzard
@Dream.corps
www www.dream.org

**DS National Logistics**
CEO/Founder: D. Scott
Scottie.d1911@gmail.com

**It's Demi's World Baby Dolls**
CEO/Founder: Demi Scott
www www.itsdemisworld.com

**Eclectikread Marketing**
CEO/Founder: Christa Newkirk
@chris_ta_da
info@eclectikread.com

**Elementz4 Designs, LLC**
CEO/Founder: Gretta Frierson
www www.elementz4designs.com
www.linktr.ee/elementz4

**engHERneered**
CEO/Founder: Christina Caldwell, PE
engherneered@gmail.com

**Enlightened Visions, Inc.**

CEO/Founder: TaNisha Fordham

✉ tanisha.fordham@gmail.com

www www.enlightenedvisions.org

**Executive Reign**

CEO/Founder: Canisha Cierra Turner

f @Executive Reign

☎ 804-605-6875

www www.executivereign.com

www www.canishacierraturner.com

**February First**

CEO/Founder: Cedric Livingston

Director/Writer: *February First: A Stride Towards Freedom*

www www.februaryfirstmovie.com

**The Flowcus Brand**

CEO/Founder: Irone Roussell

⊙ @theflowcusbrand

✉ theflowcusbrand.info@gmail.com

www www.theflowcusbrand.com

**Freeda's World Podcast**

CEO/Founder: Ritha Pierre, Esq.

⊙ @freedas_world

✉ accordingtorp@gmail.com

**DJ General Mealz**

CEO/Founder: Deitrich Armstrong

✉ dtrickarmstrong@gmail.com

## Give Black App

Co-Founder/COO: Alexus Hall

@giveblackapp

@Give Black App

@giveblackapp

www.giveblackapp.com

## Happy Hour Investors

Co-Founder/Managing Partner:
Jonathan Rivers
830 Glenwood Ave., Ste. 510-352
Atlanta, GA 30316
404-860-2288
jonathan@hhinvestors.com
www.hhinvestors.com

## Harbor Institute

CEO/Founder:
Rasheed Ali Cromwell, J.D.

@theharborinstitute

@The Harbor Institute

@harborinstitute

racromwell@theharborinstitute.com

## Harvey Wilder-Foundation

CEO/Founder: Jordan Harvey
www.hawilfoundation.org

## HBCU 101

CEO/Founder: Jahliel Thurman

@HBCU101

jahlielthurman@gmail.com

www.hbcu101.com

## The HBCU Band Experience with Christy Walker

CEO/Founder: Dr. Christy Walker

✉ christywalker57@gmail.com

🌐 www.christywalker.com

## HBCU Buzz

*(HBCU Buzz | Taper, Inc. | Root Care Health)*

CEO/Founder: Luke Lawal, Jr.

📷 @lukelawal

📘 @L & COMPANY

📱 301-221-1719

✉ lawal@lcompany.co

## HBCU Cheer Black Excellence

📷 @HBCUcheer

✉ HBCUcheerleaders@yahoo.com

## The HBCU Experience Movement, LLC

CEO/Founder: Dr. Ashley Little

📷 @_ashleyalittle

📘 @DrAshley Little

✉ thehbcuexperiencemovement@gmail.com

🌐 www.thehbcuexperiencemovement.com

## HBCU Girls Talk

CEO/Founder: TeeCee Camper

📷 @HBCUgirlstalk

✉ talkgirls@yahoo.com

## HBCU Grad

CEO/Founder: Todd Finley

📱 312-535-8511

🌐 www.hbcugraduates.com

## HBCU HUB App

*connects students directly to HBCUs*

CEO/Founder: Dr. Darrius Brooks

@hbcuhub

www.hbcuhub.us

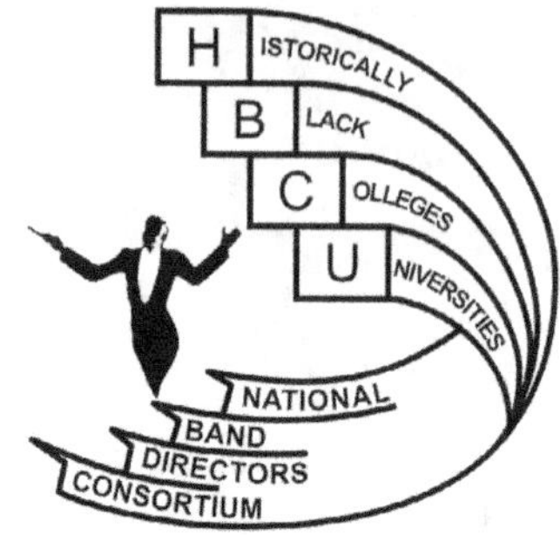

## HBCU-NBDOC

www.hbcu-nbdc.org

## HBCU Legacy Fashion

CEO/Founder: Cheylaina Fultz

@HBCULegacyFashion

@HBCULegacyFashion

contact@hbculegacyfashion.com

www.hbculegacyfashion.com

## HBCU Pride Nation

CEO/Founder: Travis Jackson

@HBCUpridenation

@HBCU Pride Nation

travispjackson@gmail.com

## HBCU Pulse

CEO/Founder: Randall Barnes

@HBCUpulse

@thehbcupulse

www.hbcupulse.com

**HBCU Recruitment Center**

CEO/Founder:

Dr. Tomisha Brock-Price

3925 N. Martin Luther King Jr. Drive Ste 209

North Las Vegas, NV 89032

✉ hbcurecruitmentcenter@gmail.com

🌐 www.hbcurecruitmentcenter.org

**HBCU Times**

CEO/Founders: David Staten, Ph. & Bridget Hollis Staten, Ph.D

📷 @HBCU_times8892

📘 @HBCU Times

✉ hbcutimes@gmail.com

**HBCU Wall Street**

CEO/Founders:

Torrence Reed & Jamerus Peyton

📘 @HBCU Wall Street

✉ info@hbcuwallstreet.com

**H.E.R. Story Podcast**

*H.E.R. Story with J. Jamison*

CEO/Founder: Janea Jamison

📷 @herstory _podcast

#Herstorymovement

**Hidden Colours**

CEO/Founder: Jahlil Witt

✉ mr.jahlilwitt@gmail.com

**Hitt Squad Ent**

CEO/Founder: Anthony Adighibe

🌐 www.hittsquadent.com

## Holistic Practitioners

CEO/Founder: Tianna Bynum

[f] @Tianna Bynum

✉ tpb33@georgetown.edu

## The Hookah Bull, LLC

*"An Elite Mobile Hookah Service"*

Owner/Operator: Roy Ector II

☎ 301-404-9735

✉ roy.ector@thehookahbull.com

🌐 www.thehookahbull.com

## ICG Marriage & Family Therapy

CEO/Founders:

　Jabari & Stephanie Walthour

[IG] @thedopesextherapist

✉ stephanie@intimacycenterga.com

🌐 www.intimacycenterga.com

## iGive

CEO/Founder: Jessica Davis

✉ igiveglobal1@gmail.com

## Johnson Capital

CEO/Founder: Marcus Johnson

[IG] @marcusdiontej

✉ marcus@johnsoncap.com

## The Jones Journey Project

CEO/Founder: Ebonee Jones

[IG] @thejonesjourneyproject

**Journee Enterprises**
CEO/Founder: Fred Whit
@frederickwjr
@Fred Whit
frederickwjr@yahoo.com

**J.Robins CPA, LLC**
CEO/Founder: Joseph Robins
@robinscpa
@jrobinscpa
9800 Line Hwy., Ste. 261
Baton Rouge, LA 70816
225-650-7306
info@jrobinscpa.com
www.jrobinscpa.com

**Kelly Collaborative Medicine**
CEO/Founder: Dr. Kathyrn Kelly
10801 Lockwood Dr., Ste. 160
Silver Spring, MD 20901
301-298-1040
www.kellymedicinemd.com

**K.Y. Turner Law Firm, PLLC**
CEO/Founder: Khanay Turner, Esq.
khanay.turner@icloud.com

**The Lab Personal and Professional Development Center, LLC**
CEO/Founder: Ebony Gourrier
www.thelabppd.com

**The Lady BUGS**
CEO/Founder: Tatiana Tinsley Dorsey
@theladybugsoffical
@HBCU Times
ladybugs_HQ@googlegroups.com

## LEMM Media Group

CEO/Founder: Cremel Nakia Burney

@cremel_the_creator

cremelburney@gmail.com

**Swing Into Their Dreams Foundation**

Co-Founders: Pamela Parker and
Lynn Demmons

swingintotheirdreams@gmail.com

www.swingintotheirdreams.com

**Like Minds Dine Productions**

CEO/Founder: Kristin J. Meyers

tokristinmeyers@gmail.com

**LK Productions**

CEO/Founder: Larry King

@lk_rrproduction

@Larry King

lkproduction@yahoo.com

**Little Publishing, LLC**

CEO/Founder: Dr. Ashley Little

@_ashleyalittle

@DrAshley Little

info@ashleyalittle.com

www.ashleylittleenterprises.com

**Lou's BluBooks**

CEO/Founder: Louis D. Roberts

202-560-7368

www.lousblubooks.com

## Lynch Law, PLLC

CEO/Founder: Chance D. Lynch, Esq.

1015A Roanoke Ave., Ste. A

Roanoke Rapids, NC 27870

252-535-1251

## MaccBoyz Entertainment

CEO/Founder: Willie Macc

@WillieMacc

www.williemacc.com

## The Marching Force

700 Emancipation Dr.

Hampton, VA 23668

www.supportthematchingforce.com

## The Marching Podcast

CEO/Founder: Joseph Beard

marchingpodcast@gmail.com

www.themarchingpodcast.com

## Marching Sport

CEO/Founder: Gerard Howard

gerardhoward@gmail.com

## McKallen Medical

CEO/Founder: Sade Stephenson,
MSN, RN, AGACNP-BC

9253 Hermosa Ave., Ste. B

Rancho Cucamonga, CA 91730

747-225-6776

mckallenmedical@gmail.com

www.mckallenmedicaltraining.com

## Minority Cannabis Business Association

President: Shanita Penny

f @MCBA.Org

🐦 @MinCannBusAssoc

in @Minority Cannabis Business Association

📠 202-681-2889

✉ info@minoritycannabis.org

www www.minoritycannabis.org

## Mills Academy

CEO/Founder: Airneica Mills

📠 662-822-6976

✉ millsacademy1@gmail.com

## MilRo Entertainment

CEO/Founder: Chevis Anderson

✉ milrosplace@yahoo.com

## MMarie Event Planning & Logistics

CEO/Founder: Megan Clay

✉ meganmclay08@gmail.com

## Mr. Anthony

CEO/Founder: Anthony Adighibe

✉ mr_anthony83@yahoo.com

## Music Greek$\Sigma$, Inc.

CEO/Founder: Jeremiah Johnson

📠 470-615-9567

✉ musicgreeks@gmail.com

www www.musicgreeks.com

**NC Dance District**

CEO/Founder: Dr. Kellye Worth Hall

@divadoc5

@Kellye Worth Hall

delta906@gmail.com

**Never2Fly2Pray**

CEO/Founder: Jeffrey Lee Sawyer

@never2fly2pray

@Jeffrey Lee

htdogwtr@yahoo.com

**NXLevel Travel (NXLTRVL)**

CEO: Hercules Conway

@herc3k

@Hercules Conway

COO: Newton Dennis

@nxlevel

@Newton Dennis

info@nxleveltravel.com

www.nxleveltravel.com

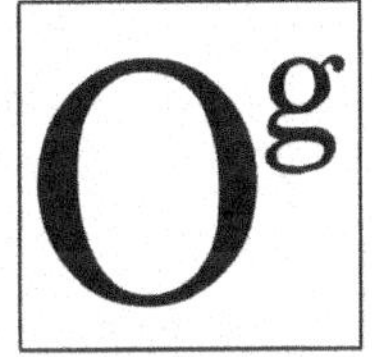

**Original Garments: Clothing Brand**

CEO/Founder: Dr. Darrius Brooks

@original.garments

*Coming Soon* (DM to purchase)

**OEDM Group**

CEO/Principal Owner: Justin Blake

@oedmgroup.com

contact@oedmgroup.com

www.oedmgroup.com

**PacketStealer Gaming**

CEO/Founder: David Matthews

✉ packetstealer@outlook.com

**PILAR**

Co-Owner: Nate Perry

⊙ @barpilar

✉ nate@pilardc.com

**The Perfect Glow**

CEO/Founder: Berrie Russell

✉ berrierussell@gmail.com

🌐 www.tpglow.com

**Props Enterprises, LLC**

CEO/Founders: Clarence & Keyanda
Satchell

✉ foreversatchell@gmail.com

**The Phoenix Professional Network**

CEO/Founder: DJavon Alston

⊙ @thephoenixnetwork757

f @DJavon Alston

✉ thephoenixnetwork757@gmail.com

**Put Up Resultz**

CEO/Founder: Kasheef Wyzard

⊙ @PutUpResultz

🌐 www.putupresultz.com

**Queen Series**

CEO/Founder: Randall Barnes

✉ aqueenseries@gmail.com

**Raggedi Luxury Durags**

CEO/Founder: Chasmin Jenkins

✉ chasminjenkins@gmail.com

**Reach Higher**

CEO/Founder: Dr. Kesha Reed

✉ info@keshareed.com

**Reed Williams,**
**A Professional Law Corporation**

CEO/Founder:

   Donald R. Williams, Jr., Esq.

9343 Tech Center Drive, Suite 165

Sacramento, CA 95826

☎ 916-281-9337

www www.reedwilliamslaw.com

**Regal PhotoBooth**

CEO/Founder: Kaleena Clarkson

✉ kaleenajp@gmail.com

**Reid Creative Solutions, LLC**

CEO/Founder: Aja Reid

☎ 919-822-2892

✉ info@reidcreativesolutions.com

www www.reidcreativesolutions.com

**Rising Stars 3lite Cheer, Dance and Tumbling**
CEO/Founders:
Dr. Ke'Shawn Roberts and
Ke'Shone Roberts
Central Texas
504-316-9325

**SC DJ WORM 803**
CEO/Founder: Jamie Brunson
@SCDJWORM803
@SC DJ Worm 803
@SCDJWORM803
@SC DJ Worm 803
scdjworm803@gmail.com
www.scdjworm803.com

**Sassy Suga Lip Service**
info@sassysuga.com
www.sassysuga.com

**Seedlinks Behavior Management**
CEO/Founder: Ryan L. Williams
1533 Marshall Street
Shreveport, LA 71101
318-626-5597

**Say Yes, LLC**
CEO/Founder: Porscha Lee Taylor
@sayyesplanners
info@sayyescareer.com
www.sayyesplanners.com

**Shani L., Relationship Enthusiast**
CEO/Founder: Shani L.Farmer
@shanilrelationshipenthusiast
info@shanilfarmer.com
www.shanilfarmer.com

## She Is Magazine

CEO/Founder: Ciara Horton

@sheisemagazine

@Ciara Horton

www.ciarasheisemagazine.com

## Sneaux Bidness

CEO/Founder: Delano Holmes

@sneaux_bidnessla

## Shonnie Murrell

BookShonnieMurrell@gmail.com

ShonnieMurrell@gmail.com

## Special Occasion

CEO/Founder: Gary Norman II

@specialoccasionlive

www.specialoccasionlive.com

## The Silent Majority

CEO/Founder: Rodney Henry

757-239-1039

www.dearsummerbbq.com

## Social Status PR

CEO/Founder: Ray Cunningham

@SocialStatusPR

**Southern University A&M College**

801 Harding Blvd.

Baton Rouge, LA 70807

225-771-4500

**Southern University Alumni Federation**

124 Roosevelt Steptoe Dr.

Baton Rouge, LA 70807

225-771-4200

sualumni@sualumni.org

**Springbreak Watches (SPGBK)**

CEO/Founder: Kwame Molden

@SPGBK

@Kwame Molden

info@springbreakwatches.com

**Stamp'd Travel**

CEO/Founder:

Jocelyn Hadrick Alexander

@jocehadyou

jocelyn.h.alexander@gmail.com

www.stampdtravel.com

**Strategic Consulting, LLC**

CEO/Founder:

Desiree' C. Cotton-Turner, Esq.

4917 S. Sherwood Forest Blvd.

Baton Rouge, LA 70817

225-371-3638

**Success and Religion**

CEO/Founder: Micheal Taylor

successismyreligion@gmail.com

**Sugar Top Spirit & Beverage Co.**

CEO/Founder: Terri White

@sugartopspirits

@sugartopspirits

tl.white412@gmail.com

www.sugartopspirits.com

**SwagHer**

Vice President of Sales / Marketing:

Jarmel Roberson

@swaghermagazine

jroberson@swagher.net

www.swagher.net

**Tavia Botanicals**

CEO/Founder: Kayonca Riggs

drkayriggs@gmail.com

**TLW Photography**

CEO/Founder: Taylor Whitehead

mrknowitall91@aol.com

**Uplift Clothing Apparel**

CEO/Founder: Jermaine Simpson

@upliftclothingapparel

www.upliftclothingapparel.com

**Upward Path**

CEO/Founder:

Cameron Chalmers Dupree

@upwardpathtc

contact@upwardpathtc.com

www.upwardpathtc.com

## The Urban Learning & Leadership Center, Inc.

President/Co-Founder:

John W. Hodge, Ed.D

✉ jhodge@ulleschools.com

## Urban Millennial Lifestyle

CEO/Founder: Nolita R. Pore

⊙ @themonalita

@fitlikelita

✉ contact@themonalita.com

🌐 www.themonalita.com

The Vernon Group
Cooperative Solutions

## The Vernon Group Cooperative Solutions

CEO/Founder: Anthony V. Stevens

⊙ @investednu

✉ info@vernongroupllc.com

## Vision Tree, LLC

CEO/Founder: Dr. Jorim Reed

⊙ @upwardpathtc

✉ visiontreellc@gmail.com

## Vision Unlimited, LLC

CEO/Founder: Kirby Denise Wilson

⊙ @Kirby_Denise_

🅵 @Kirby Denise

✉ info@teamvisionunlimited.com

🌐 www.teamvisionunlimited.com

**VJR Real Estate**

CEO/Founder: Victor Collins, Jr.

@vjrtherealtor

vic@thevjrgroup.com

**Yard Talk 101**

CEO/Founder: Jahliel Thurman

@YardTalk101

www.yardtalk101.com

We Are Educated, Inc.

**We Are Educated, Inc.**

CEO/Founder: Ayanna Spivey

@ayannaceleste

ayanna.spivey@yahoo.com

**Yardopoly**

CEO/Founder: Ray Cunningham

@Yardopoly

yardopoly@gmail.com

www.thegamecrafter.com
(*search: Yardopoly*)

**Yard Stubs**

CEO/Founder: Cremel Burney

@YardStubs

partnerships@yardstubs.com

www.yardstubs.com

**Zoom Technologies, LLC**

CEO/Founder: Torrence Reed

@torrencereed3

support@zoom-technologies.com